The Mountain Goat Chronicles

By Mario Locatelli*

To Gene & Nora

Also Known As "The Montana Mountain Goat"

Mario Locatelli

The Mountain Goat Chronicles

By Mario Locatelli*

Also Known As "The Montana Mountain Goat"

Library of Congress Number: 2008938178

ISBN: 1-931291-72-1

Published in the United States of America

First Edition

ALL RIGHTS RESERVED
No part of this publication may be reproduced, stored in a retrieval system, or transmitted in any form or by any means without the prior written permission of the copyright owner or the publisher.

STONEYDALE PRESS PUBLISHING COMPANY
523 Main Street • P.O. Box 188
Stevensville, Montana 59870
Phone: 406-777-2729
Email: stoneydale@montana.com

DEDICATION

This book is dedicated to my daughter Carlene.

I've met a lot of nice people in my life, but she was tops. God sent me an angel from heaven which I believe she still remains. She was always ready to help someone in need, she is always in my thoughts . . . I miss her . . .

Mario Locatelli's namesake, the Rocky Mountain Goat, photos taken in the high country of the Bitterroot Range in western Montana by Mario himself.

TABLE OF CONTENTS

Dedication 3
Foreword 7
Chapter One
The Beginning – Italy to America 9
Chapter Two
Buried Alive, by Cathy Locatelli 23
Chapter Three
Search and Rescue 29
Chapter Four
Hiking For Charity 37
Chapter Five
The Bitterroot – Rivers and Mountains 43
Chapter Six
A Walk With Mario, by Cathy Locatelli 49
Chapter Seven
Hunting In The Bitterroot 55
Color Photo Section 57
Chapter Eight
Keeping The Mountains Clean 75
Chapter Nine
Bears 79
Chapter Ten
Pack Animals – Mules and Horses 81
Chapter Eleven
Pesky, Pesky Wood Ticks 83
Chapter Twelve
Alaska Moose Hunt 85
Chapter Thirteen
Kilimanjaro 103
Chapter Fourteen
The Old Goat Climbs Denali, by Cathy Locatelli 109

Chapter Fifteen
Climbing McKinley *113*
Chapter Sixteen
Mount Everest *119*
Chapter Seventeen
Family and Friends *121*
Epilogue *135*

FOREWORD

When my father told me that he was going to publish his autobiography, I asked him what he hoped to accomplish with the book. He said that many people have told him that he has inspired them and maybe his story would reach more. He appears to be ageless, his body a specimen of never-ending energy.

I think this book has more to offer. I think all readers will identify with something in his story. We all have hardships and triumphs which my father has shared, but this story is about a young boy born in another country with U.S. citizenship that discovers a talent that enables him to scale more than church steeples and mountain tops. He embraced the opportunities that our country had to offer and achieved success and good health despite the challenges of language and lack of a high school education.

He told me once that he didn't realize there were options in life other than to work hard and have a family. He feels that he could have been a great mountain climber if he hadn't had children. I took it personal at first, but after considering the truth of the matter I realized that he still doesn't believe that he "is" a great mountain climber; and I have to wonder what it will take to make him feel that he is. What would it be like to spend your life climbing mountains, one step in front of the other, over and over again. What desire drives his body forward past exhaustion?

I have wondered how he has been able to hike and climb the thousands of places he has been without serious injury. I think this book should come with a warning label: "Do not try this". The miles he goes with little water, little food, no rope, survival gear or first-aid supplies. He travels so light that he takes the labels off his pack. For him to accomplish what he has in the mountains, I think he has to concentrate and focus on his path, not the stress and trouble on his mind.

This book is a chapter in my father's spiritual journey. I hope this story reveals more to the reader than the obvious and that it will encourage not only reflection but will inspire to go after what seems impossible. I believe my father will evolve and see himself as a great mountain climber. I have seen the sparkle in his eyes when he tells me about what he has seen; he has taught me that comfort of bedding down on the loam of a mountain's back; and how to find my way home. For this I am grateful and perpetually inspired

*Cathy Locatelli
Hamilton, Montana
September 22, 2008*

Chapter 1

THE BEGINNING – ITALY TO AMERICA

My grandfather, Pietro Locatelli, at the age of eighteen, and his three brothers, came from Italy to America in 1895. He settled in Boulder Creek, California, and got a job as a foreman for a logging outfit. At the age of twenty-two he went back to Italy to marry Teresa Salvi, my grandmother's sister. They had two boys. The first one was delivered by a midwife. Back in those days, it was common for a husband to observe the delivery by a midwife so he could learn what and how to do it at the next birth. My grandfather then delivered the second child and it went well. However, it was not so with the third child. The mother and baby both died during delivery. Grandfather then wrote to the sister of his deceased wife, Caterina, my grandmother, and asked her to come to America to get married and help him raise the two boys so they would have a mother. They then had another child by the name of Battista on November 3, 1906, who was my father.

In addition to taking care of the children, she had to cook for the family as well as the logging crew. As far as I know, she was the only woman there in the camp, which was very rough, and she had to put up with a lot. She became very depressed and was homesick – she knew she had to get back to Italy. She could not handle this hardship any longer.

My grandfather promised her he would follow her back to Italy later on. He never made good on his promise; nor did he ever send her any money to help her with raising the children. When she left, she was pregnant again. The second child between her and my grandfather was born in Italy; his name was Giuseppe. The two children by her sister were named Oresti and Adolfo. They all grew up in Italy with the help of her family.

Eventually my father got married in Italy. His wife's name was Angela Locatelli, but no relation. My father and mother had twelve children – four boys and eight girls. I was number three. Being that my father was born in the USA, he was an American citizen and so we all, brothers and sisters, ended up with dual citizenship. In order not to lose our American citizenship, we had to come to America before we were twenty-one years of age.

Growing up in Italy as a child was not an easy life. We all had daily chores to do. My oldest sister, Giannina, had to help my mother around the house. My oldest brother, Battista, spent most of his time with my father. My father was a very ambitious man, a wheeler and dealer in many things. In Berbenno, a small town of about 2,000 people in northern Italy, my dad was the first person to own a truck. It ran on wood. In the back of the cab was a big wood stove and it had to be kept stoked up with wood to keep it running. I remember the stove being red hot! Every so often my father stopped to clean out the filters or the truck would quit running if they were plugged up.

We always had a couple of cows, chickens, rabbits and a few hogs which kept us in meat and milk. I was mostly in charge of taking care of the livestock, and I enjoyed it. When I was ten years old, I would milk two cows twice a day. My brother, Pete, who was three years younger, helped me with some of the chores. Most of the families had a cow or two and a few other animals. People would plant big gardens. Most of the time, the cows would be in the barn and tied up to a manger.

The climate was humid. The farmers were able to raise two crops of hay, which were cut with a scythe. The scythes needed to be sharpened often so they would beat them on a anvil with a special hammer. Every so often they would be touched up with a stone which was kept in a cow's horn on a belt around your waist filled half with water and vinegar. The hay would be raked with a homemade wooden rake to dry. Toward the evening it would be piled in cones in the field so if it should rain during the night it would not get so wet. The next morning the hay piles would be taken apart again and dried out some more. This was repeated until the hay was totally dry. It would then be put into the loft of the barn. It was carried on a person's back with a sled-like carrier. The kids up in the loft would stomp on the hay to pack it down.

To feed the cows, the hay would be cut with a special blade into chunks and then thrown down into the mangers. In the summer the cows would graze on the hillsides for a few hours and they had to be watched since there were no fences. Afterward they were led to a fountain for drinking. Not everyone could afford a bull so you would bring your cow to a farmer who had one. For a small fee you had your cow bred. After the calf was born, it stayed only for a short time with the mother and then would be butchered.

The excess milk was brought to a community hall where a man would weigh it and keep track of the amounts each family brought in. After so many gallons were brought in, a day would be designated and one of the family would go to the community hall and help the man make cheese. You would then receive a wheel of cheese. Also, every time you would bring in a bucket of milk, you would then bring a bucket of whey back which would be fed to the pigs.

In the fall when the leaves fell from the trees, we would rake the leaves and put them in special baskets. We carried them on our backs back to the barn where they were used for bedding. The cow manure was picked up with pitchforks and piled outside the barn. In the spring it was hauled out in baskets on our backs into the field for fertilizing where it was raked out. After a month or so, the chunks that had not dissolved were raked together and brought back to the barn to be recycled with the fresh manure.

The urine went into a concrete septic tank and was scooped up with buckets on a rainy day and spread in the fields. Every family had a garden with vegetables, grain and fruit trees. People pretty much lived off of the land. Some of the men would go to Switzerland or France during the summer months to work and come home for a few months during the winter. My brother, Battista, went to work when he was fifteen in Switzerland and worked for a logger dragging trees with a tractor.

In our area we had two radical groups – one was the Fascists and the other group was the Partisans. At times they came into confrontation with each other and it ended with killings. One particular fellow, a Fascist by the name of Barbo, which means "The Bearded One", was a big braggart. A bunch of guys from the other side went to his house in the middle of the night, took him out to a wooded place, and shot him. Most people were Fascists but they kept it quiet for fear that they might also be killed. Since my folks had a small restaurant and bar, plus a few rental rooms, the Partisans would show up unexpectedly and demand to be fed and housed. I am not sure if they ever paid for the accommodations. Whenever my father would hear through the grapevine that the group was coming, he went into hiding for a few days since he was a Fascist and he was nervous they would do to him what they had done to Barbo.

My dad was one of the few that had a radio and he liked to listen to the news. One day, some of these radicals came into the bar and grabbed the radio without asking or paying for it, and left. Someone made a whole bunch of homemade soap for us and my older sister and I were sent off by my father to the neighboring villages to sell pieces of soap. My dad instructed us to stop at all the establishments along to way to see if we might locate his stolen radio. He was also hoping the soap selling would turn out to be a good business. One time we came home in the evening after we had sold all the soap and my father demanded the money. My sister was in charge of the wallet but could not find it. She had lost it along the way. Needless to say, my father was furious and hit her with the carrying basket in the behind. Luckily, the wallet was later returned by some honest citizen who had found it. We never did recover the radio.

On Easter Sunday, the town folk of Berbenno and other little towns around there would hike up to Saint Pietro, a small mountain with a church and a bell tower on top, where Easter Mass was held. Afterward the children gathered Easter eggs and played. My father would send me there with a mule and a small barrel of wine, including a spigot. I would sell the wine to folks after church. Everyone would be sitting around and have a good time. Good food would also be on hand. By nightfall some got a little tipsy, but most everyone would then head for home.

My father was always trying to figure out how to make a fast buck. Occasionally, he would buy a parcel of standing forest from a private party. He would then hire someone to cut the trees down with an axe and handsaw them into lengths of six and seven feet. Nothing was wasted; even the wood chips would be gathered. The branches were bundled and used for kindling. Since there were no roads in the forest going up into the mountains, the men would set up a cable as close as possible to where the wood was cut. An anchor would be put into the ground and the cable would be hooked up on it. Another anchor with a spool would be set up close to where the wood would be loaded onto horse-drawn carts. It was a very touchy project to keep the cable tight and could be quite dangerous. I helped bring up the little pulleys in a sack which were then attached to the cable. The bundles of wood would be hooked onto the pulleys and then sent down the hill. There, the wood was loaded on the carts. We kept some of the wood for our own use and the rest was sold. The bread maker would buy the bundled limbs of wood to heat up the bread oven.

At that time, most people had no running water. Our nearest water source was a spring about a half a mile from where we lived. The water ran into a small cement pond the size of a bathtub. We hauled the water by carrying two buckets – one on each end of a pole – over our backs to the house. A pipe connected to the outflow of the spring ran the water into the buckets. The cows, horses, mules and goats were herded to the spring for drinking every day. The water from the small pond would run into a bigger one which had a slanted cement rim. The women would bring the dirty clothes to the pond and do their laundry there with homemade soap. The slanted edge was used as a washboard. The overflow of the water would end up in a ditch.

The house in which my family lived was four stories high. My parents rented a few rooms in the summertime to folks from the city, and we had only one bathroom in the house. For washing dishes and use of water for the toilet, we had a tank in the attic which caught the water running off of the roof when it rained. We were also the only ones in this little town to have a telephone.

My father was very strict – he kept us busy with chores and we never were allowed to play. I was afraid of him because he had a bad temper, especially after drinking. Sometimes he would send me out into the countryside with a message to a neighbor. He would speak very fast and I was so nervous and scared that I could not understand him. I would go to my mother and ask her to find out what my father wanted me to do. After she found out, she would explain it to me in a gentle way. My mother was very good. She raised thirteen children with the help of my grandmother. She was very affectionate to all of us kids. My parents were very fortunate to have my grandmother living with us. She was such a great help around the house. Late at night she would go to the spring with a basket of clothes on her shoulder to wash. She helped with the cooking. But, she was very unhappy. I would see her crying at times. She died of a broken heart and was only fifty-four years old.

Our meals were very modest. In the mornings our meal consisted of warm milk, a little coffee as well as stale bread added to the milk. For lunch, the main meal was vegetables, a little cheese and bread. Once in a while we would butcher a rabbit or chicken. For supper we always had rice, beans, or pasta soup, sometimes with salted pork. Seldom would we buy meat from the butcher, and only then meat for boiling. Before the butcher would slaughter an animal he would want the customers to commit to buying a certain amount of the meat so he would get rid of it since there was no refrigeration. Nothing was wasted – lungs and kidneys were saved for soup and from the stomach lining we made tripe. Sometimes the butcher would come to my father very upset and whining that he had not gotten rid of all the meat because his customers did not show up. My dad would then take some of it off of his hands for our own use.

The school system in Italy was quite different than in the United States. I went to elementary school from 8:00 a.m. to 1:00 p.m. five days a week. You learned the basics. The teachers ran very disciplined classes and would not put up with any nonsense. Sometimes you would get your hand slapped with a stick, and very quickly the teacher had your attention again. We had no lunch program. We ate lunch when we came home. Neither did we have bus service or sports. Most kids were done with school by the age of eleven or twelve. This is all the schooling I had. When I was finished with school, I had to work for my father. I was almost sixteen years old when my father decided to send my older brother, older sister, myself, and two cousins to America.

My father took us to the ship in Genova and we sailed to New York; my mother took it very hard seeing us leave. We were traveling third class and it took eleven days to reach New York. Our sleeping quarters were in the bottom of the ship in bunk beds. For a couple of days the sea was very rough and on one occasion while we were eating, the plates began to slide off the tables. My cousin, who was the same age as I, was sick all eleven days and never came up to eat. We told him that he would die if he did not eat, but it did not do any good. It was an adventure for us kids. We enjoyed watching the dolphins swimming along the ship.

When we arrived in New York and saw the Statue of Liberty, we were in awe. Then, of course, we had to go to Customs. Since no one in our group spoke English, it was somewhat difficult to communicate with the Customs officer who was checking us out. We had brought a wheel of cheese along which we were to give to one of our relatives in California. When the Customs officer opened the box, what a surprise! Only a little chunk was left. We knew now how my cousin survived eleven days in the belly of the ship. We had a good laugh.

We had also brought a box with a few machetes for our relatives. The Customs man was not sure what to make of this. He took one out and held it behind his head, as if to say; "Are you planning on killing someone with this?" Fortunately, an English-speaking Italian man came over to help us out and explained what these knives were for. They would be used strictly for cutting limbs and trees and brush. The Customs man let us go through.

My oldest sister, Giannina, was looking after us and had enough money along to buy one meal for us on the train to California. My grandfather was supposed to have sent some money for our travel, but we never did see it. The train trip to California took four days. When we became hungry we went to the dining car. The colored waiter showed up to take our order. Since we could not speak English, we motioned with our hands that we wanted to eat. We pointed to the food at the next table where people were eating. He got the message and we received food after a little while. On the table was bowl filled with sugar cubes and a bottle of ketchup. When the waiter showed up, he was very surprised to see what we had done. He realized that we must have been very hungry – nothing was left!

I remember that there were many soldiers on the train. Since I was pretty small for my age, the guys would come by with popcorn and chocolate and say to me, "Here, Sonny." I always shared the goodies with the rest of the gang.

When we arrived in Oakland, California, a friend of a distant relative of ours picked us up. I stayed with two second cousins. Since they had many fruit trees and they needed to be pruned, they showed me how to do it. This was a job I was stuck with for several months, and I made only $1.00 a day, room and board. During the day, my cousins were working at odd jobs someplace else because they could not make a living off their small ranch. My uncle, who was my grandfather's brother, was a very nice man. His wife had dementia. Their little ranch was about ten miles from Santa Cruz.

At that time I was staying with Richard, a cousin, and his wife in their small house. Richard was thirty-three years old and he had a bad temper. They had two daughters – ages ten and eleven. Another cousin, Frank, age twenty-seven, and his wife lived in Santa Cruz. They had a couple of small children. Frank was different from Richard – a very compassionate man. After I was there a couple of months, they planned a family gathering. It was held at the old parents' house. We all had a very good meal. One of my girl cousins asked me what English I had learned so far. I told her some words that Richard had taught me, but they turned out to be mostly dirty words. My cousin was very embarrassed and left the house.

When I was working in the orchard all day long, I started to feel homesick and very down. In the morning I would see the bus coming by to pick up the children for school and I would still be in the orchard when the bus would bring the children back. I should have been on the bus going to school to learn.

The only event I looked forward to and enjoyed was going to the movies on Saturdays with Richard and his family. Richard had picked up a pair of used Army boots for me which were way too big. I ended up with athlete's foot and did not know what it was. I showed my feet to my sister and she was shocked at the condition of my feet and picked up some powder from the drugstore. Afterward, I got rid of the boots.

Meanwhile, my sister had gotten a job at the Levi factory in Santa Cruz where they made jeans. My brother, Battista, went to work driving tractors for a group of Italian farmers who raised a lot of broccoli and Brussels sprouts. After three months, my sister lined me up with a job at the Levi factory as a bundle boy. I had to carry the bundles to the women who were sewing the jeans.

We rented an old house and we all lived there and chipped in. It was very hard for my sister. She worked all day at the factory and then fixed a meal for all of us in the evening.

The following winter I went to work picking sprouts to make a little more money. Some days were so miserable; the wind and the rain would come off the ocean and my hands and fingers would get very cold. Two other cousins of mine had come to the States six months earlier than we. The older of the two got a job at a cement quarry plant 20 miles up the coast in a little town called Davenport. He worked in the hills at the quarry. They were paying pretty good money for those days – $3.40/hour. My brother ended up working there, as well as my cousin, Salvatore, who had come with us to the USA. Adolfo, my other cousin, worked for a packing plant. He packed Brussels sprouts and broccoli. He also was very handy at fixing up and keeping the machinery running.

Two more of my uncles had come over from Italy; Adolfo, the father of my cousins Adolfo and Salvatore; and Oresti, the father of Fiorindo and Battista, who had come over six months before we did. They all went to work in the quarry. My cousin, Battista, and I wanted to work at the quarry also but they would not hire anyone who weighed under 150 lbs because they would have to be able to handle a ninety-pound jackhammer. We both weighed around 130 pounds. Of course, I had gained weight since I weighed only eighty-eight pounds when I came to the United States.

One day, the quarry went on strike because people wanted more money for their work. In those days, the owner was still the boss of his own company and he informed the workers that they either came back to work or were fired. My uncle, Adolfo, went back to work along with the rest of the Locatellis. My uncle told me and my cousin they were in need of workers and might just hire us now – and we did get hired.

Some of the workers eventually returned to the job but they were very angry at all of my relatives because they had stayed on the job. They were very upset and angry at my cousin and I because we were hired. They called us "scabs". My cousin and I decided to show them that we could do just as good of a job as they and we ended up drilling more holes than they did. We would put one of our legs over the handle of the jackhammer, which gave it more pressure, and the drilling went faster. Each driller had a helper and he would hand us the steel as we drilled deeper until twenty-one feet was reached. Every evening the helpers would carry the bits back down to the shop and someone would sharpen them.

One day, when I had my leg over the jackhammer, the steel bit broke. It bounced off and hit the big toe on my left leg. It took one-half an inch off the end of my big toe. I was afraid I would lose my job so I did not say anything to the foreman. When I came home, I had a lot of blood in my shoe and it was hurting big time. This happened about three-and-a-half years after I had started working there, and five months after I had gotten married. My wife helped with cleaning the wound and disinfected it. I was limping for a few days, but managed to go back to my job the next morning. My cousin and I worked there for six years.

After that, my cousin and I got a job with the City of Santa Cruz packing garbage. We were getting better wages, which was good since I had started a family. I had two girls at the time – Cathy and Carlene. Packing garbage was very hard in those days. Each of us had an aluminum can with a big handle that held three household-size cans. We packed the big garbage cans on our backs and brought them to the truck to be dumped. Each truck had three to four guys picking up and dumping. We had a certain route and number of houses to service each day. Every day a different section of town; five days a week. The sooner we would be finished with our route, the sooner we could go home. We were young tough guys in those days. Running and picking up the trash at 5:00 in the morning, and we would be done at about 11:00.

I met a few individuals that had some properties out in the boonies and wanted their forests thinned out. I would go there in the afternoons and work for four or five hours cutting trees down for firewood. I bought a truck with a flatbed on which I could haul two cords of wood. My brother Battista's mother-in-law owned some land outside of Santa Cruz and she allowed me to stack the wood there for drying. I sold it in the winter. I worked packing garbage in the mornings and cutting wood in the afternoons for three years. These were the hardest years of my life.

I also had bought an old house on a big lot in downtown Santa Cruz for $7,000. I made a lot of improvements on the house. I also put a big garden in the back and raised a few rabbits and chickens. By then, I had acquired quite a few customers who bought wood from me, so I quit the garbage hauling and went out on my own. I eventually sold my house downtown and doubled my money. I was twenty-six years old and never worked for anyone else again.

I bought a place about five miles outside of Santa Cruz with an old house on two acres. I also bought several wooded pieces of land in the mountains. With an old bulldozer which I had acquired, I was putting roads into the properties. I got rid of the flatbed truck and bought a dump truck, which would hold two cords of wood. All through the spring and summer I cut wood, but only the hardwood and I would leave the redwood. I would usually make two trips a day. I would go home for lunch and bring one load home. My two helpers helped me split and load the wood. In the evening I would bring another load home.

By the end of fall, my two acres would be full of stacked wood, four feet high. During the winter I delivered the wood to customers. I sold about 600 cords of wood a year and used to get $35 a delivered cord. During the summer I would also sell green wood directly from the woods to customers and I received $50 for two delivered cords. It was a lot of hard work but I made a good living. Occasionally, I would remove trees from people's yards which they wanted to get rid of. I had Santa Cruz pretty much sewed up in the wood business. The only other Italian fellow who was in the same business had retired. Four or five cousins of mine who saw that I was doing very good also got into the wood cutting and hauling business. There were about 500 Locatellis living between Santa Cruz and Boulder Creek, so when people would call me to find out about wood, they asked which of the Locatellis I was. I would answer them, "I am the original!" At times it would get pretty hectic between all of the Locatellis selling wood.

I then bought an old track loader with a big bucket in front. Bob

Burns, who was married to my sister Marcella at the time, was working at a machine shop in San Jose. He was very ingenious and made me a heavy-duty tilt trailer so I could haul my loader behind the truck. I started to do some odd jobs for people.

My brother, Pete, was in the landscaping business, and once in a while he would have some work for me. He knew of someone that needed an old house to be demolished, so I tore down my first house and I thought to myself, "This could be fun." But, there was a lot of competition in this line of work.

I talked it over with my wife and we decided to move to Oregon. We rented a house on the outskirts of Salem and I parked my loader next to the road with a sign – "For Hire". I saw in the newspaper where the City of Salem was advertising for a bid to remove several houses. I went to see about it and found out that I needed to have a contractor's license. I went to get the license and put in a bid. I actually got a few of the houses to be torn down.

There was another wrecking contractor in Salem. He had about fifteen to twenty guys working for him. He also had a big salvage yard. The salvage was usually retrieved before he demolished the old houses. When he heard about me, he asked me if I wanted to go to work for him. I told him that I would not work for him, but if he would throw a little business to me that I would let him have all the salvage.

My old machinery was starting to give me some problems and it also was too dangerous to use it for demolishing work. I went to the Caterpillar dealer in Portland to see about buying a Cat. I traded the old piece of equipment in and put some money down on a brand new loader, Model 951. It had a big bucket, a canopy, and a winch on the back. It was ideal for this kind of work. The machine weighed 26,000 pounds. I made payments on the rest of the purchase price, which was $29,000. My work flourished and I was getting many jobs.

I had two ten-wheelers with twenty-foot dump boxes which could haul an entire house and foundation away in three loads. I hired a man to drive the trucks for me. While he was taking a load to a private dump ten miles away, I would fill up the other truck. Some days we would take out three average-size houses and dump them. Occasionally, I would get some big jobs from the Urban Renewal Program. A whole block of buildings in the old part of the city had to be taken out for clean-up. These jobs would be put out on bids so other folks could participate. Some bids came in from as far away as Portland and San Francisco. I ended up getting most of the jobs because I could do it for less since I did not have a high overhead.

Once I had several three-to-four-story downtown buildings for demolition. I needed to hire a contractor with a crane and a steel ball who would smash down the buildings so I could get in with my machine for the clean-up. This contractor had a bigger machine than I did, so I would hire him occasionally to help me with some of my many jobs. I actually loved this kind of work, but it was very dirty and dusty. With all the work I was getting, I ended up hiring more workers and I just ran around trying to keep the operation going. This was a big headache for me and I did not want to deal with it. I also did not want to ruin my health due the constant dust I was inhaling. I turned the business over to my driver and his brother-in-law. They bought my trucks and machine. I was in the business only six years but had made quite a bit of money.

Early in his efforts to climb the world's highest peaks, Mario began a tradition of getting a photograph of him standing on his head just after he reached the summit to prove that his feet had been higher at that site than anyone else who'd made the climb. This photo shows Mario on Wheeler Peak, the highest in New Mexico.

On a trip with my family to Montana, we fell in love with the Bitterroot Valley and in 1970 I decided to buy a 160-acre ranch and move to Montana. My wife, however, was not happy out on the ranch and we were having marriage problems. We ended up divorcing.

Divorces are expensive and I lost half of the ranch in the settlement. I started going to the bars trying to find happiness, but it was not for me. I knew I had to find something different to do. I put on my hiking boots and started hiking the drainages on the west side of the Bitterroot Valley – right in my own back yard. I began hiking, and hunting, in the mountains around me. I also joined the local Search and Rescue unit, which I was in for twenty years and I was the head of its rock climbing team for ten years. I enjoyed my hiking very much.

I usually went hiking a couple of times a week. When I was on top of the peaks, I felt like a soaring eagle and I started to feel good again. I hiked all the canyons and ridges on the west side. Then I thought, "Wouldn't it be nice if I would hike the whole west side from Lolo South to Nez Perce Pass into Idaho."

It took me a few years to do them all – the canyons and ridges – all forty of them. Some days I would put in between twelve and fourteen hours hiking and be pretty tired when I came home. During that time, I developed good hiking skills for climbing the rocks. A few times some individuals would come along with me. After awhile, however, nobody wanted to walk with me any more because I was too fast for them.

I did see some beautiful, rugged country on my hikes, as well as wildlife and many wildflowers. I always had my camera along and took pictures. Looking up from the bottom of the valley to the tops of the mountains, you don't see the beauty up there; and it is a like a different world looking down into the valleys from way up high. In the winter I would alpine ski on the westside slopes. Hiking in the summer and skiing in the winter kept me pretty fit.

Mario on top of Mount Adams in Washington state, with Mount Hood in Oregon in the background.

Chapter 2

BURIED ALIVE
(Told by Cathy Locatelli, Mario's daughter)

    There is one brief moment in time when a decision can be changed and the previous outcome will never be known, such as a brief moment when you discover how close Death is to continued Life. Mario Locatelli and Richard "Dick" Robertson have tried to change a decision they made a few years ago in their minds hundreds of times, attempting to relieve themselves of a horrifying experience – being consumed by an avalanche. As you experience their story, you may find yourself asking the same questions. What would you have done?
    On February 28, 1981, Mario and Dick planned their first back country ski trip together. They became friends during their common interest in bow hunting. Dick is a Bow Designer and Craftsman. Mario's love of the sport and admiration for Dick's craft initiated several hunting and camping trips. Dick had alpine skied, but had not really experienced "bushwhacking"– using a combination cross country/downhill type ski. The ski is 150-160 cm., cable bindings, the boots are heavy leather mountaineering type, and the poles long with large baskets to help give leverage in the powder snow.
    The peak south of Ward Mountain was their destination, elevation of about 9,000 feet. Lost Horse Road gave access to the Observation Point Road, which was driven until the snow depth would not give further passage. Dick left his truck parked there, equipment was put on, backpacks carried their provisions. They began the climb about 7:30 a.m. The sunrise promised warmer temperatures and beautiful landscapes.
    The two men enjoyed their climb, sharing hunting stories, and reminiscing about the past mountain lion season, as they crossed the

path of lion tracks. They estimated the lion's size and had him located and treed in their minds within moments of the track sighting. As they arrived at the Saddle, which is approximately 500 feet below the peak, they decided to take a break and have some lunch. The views of the surrounding canyons, such as the North Fork of Lost Horse, were spectacular that day. They decided to leave their packs there to be free of the additional weight, as they were just going to ski to the peak and ski back down the outskirts of the bowl to retrieve their packs.

As they began the incline, Mario discussed with Dick that this bowl was a potential avalanche area. It was best for them to ski the ridge on the way back down to avoid the danger of fracturing the snow loose from the steep slope. Mario had attended an Avalanche Course, and was a member of the Search and Rescue, so he had some knowledge of the potential damage that a large accumulation of snow could do on a steep slope on a warm day, early in the afternoon.

Once the peak was reached, a few minutes of rest were taken, and again the even more incredible view was enjoyed. They took off from the top, hooting and hollering as they enjoyed carving their turns in the deep snow. They had not gone very far when the slope began to get very steep. Dick was unsure of his ability to maneuver his way down this portion. Mario looked over the terrain, he saw several large rock outcroppings not far from them so he decided that the best route at this point would be to circle these rocks and get back on the ridge. He realized then how much snow had blown into this big bowl. He estimated it to be ten to fifteen feet deep. They took off trying to get around this steep part. As Mario was just about to reach the ridge, he stopped and looked up to see Dick just about twenty-five yards away. Just as Dick stopped, Mario saw a two to four-foot fracture of the snow breaking away from the slope just above Dick, and then the entire mountainside let go. The snow was like a huge concrete slab that began to break up as it picked up speed. The two men were picked up and carried like a particle of dust in the midst of the all-encompassing roar.

Panic struck Dick as Mario fell out of his view as they both were forced into the unexpected trip down the mountainside. Dick's skis were taken out from underneath him in a rotating flurry. He found himself quickly on his side. He began to anticipate the fact that this could be the end for him. He wouldn't have a story to take home to his family that evening of his day adventure to the peak. He struggled with all his ability against the overwhelming blocks of snow. He was being carried into the depths of this unforgiving force to a frozen tomb. He hit something that felt like a steel wall. His terror increased as he realized that he could not even move his fingers to make himself an airspace to breath. His icy prison was a black that he never knew existed in the color spectrum. He then knew that he would never see or feel the brightness of the beautiful sun. His world turned to nothing.

Mario tried to ski the tops of the racing, frozen river of snow. The momentum overtook his balance, he fell on his back, and be began to swim in an attempt to stay afloat. His instincts told him that it wasn't his time to take his trip to the Lord's side, it just couldn't be his time to die yet. He and his wife, Doris, had a child on the way; he was needed here. Three trees were coming up, he thought they could save him if he could just reach them. He was traveling about fifty miles per hour by then; if he had not been successful, the snow would have quickly overtaken and buried him. They would have been his demise.

The avalanche came to a stop as quickly as it began except for a few tumbling balls of snow that came to rest in their chosen places. The entire mountainside reverted back to being as quiet as it had been just minutes before, like nothing had ever happened. The landscape showed otherwise. The entire bowl looked like a rock slide made of ice blocks. A huge accumulation of snow was backed up at the bottom.

Mario didn't feel any major injury. His fingers were bleeding from the nails that were torn from his fingers as he successfully swam above the moving ice. He looked anxiously up the slope in hopes of seeing his friend. He wanted him to be safe more than anything he had ever desired in his life. He called out for him, no answer. He saw a ski pole, broken in two about 100 yards above him. He quickly realized the one ski that remained with him and began to climb the frozen rubble. By now, he knew that Dick was buried; fear and agony went through his body as he began to think of how he could never forgive himself for bringing Dick with him that day if he couldn't leave with him alive.

He scanned the bright white terrain for any glimpse of another color, as he scrambled toward the broken ski pole. He caught a glimpse of a two-inch patch of cloth next to a tree that looked like Dick's pants. He began to dig around the patch – a ski came into view. He released the ski and began to shovel the snow that was compressed as hard as cement.

It soon became clear that Dick was wrapped around the tree at a 45 degree angle. He was packed in so tight no air could reach him. As the hole became deeper, some of the snow that he had just dug out would fall back into the hole. His arms and back were burning with the ache of his fatigued muscles. His endurance and strength were weakening. As he was on his knees digging, he prayed, "Dear God, give me the strength to get Dick out in time!" He no sooner got the words out of his mouth, when he felt something softer. He knew that it had to be Dick's head. He began to dig with his hands to free him. It took about another ten minutes to break the icy mask away from Dick's face, which was blue – no sign of life.

Mario lifted his friend with all his might out of the hole, ready to resuscitate him. No time to worry about broken bones, Dick had to have air. Then Dick began to cough, choke and vomit. His lungs burned with fire, but what a glorious sound it was! The first words from Dick were, "Am I still in the hole?" Mario replied, "No Dick, I love you, I love you!" They embraced in the most thankful warmth two men can share. Less than a half hour earlier maneuvering a mountainside, now thankful to have survived that moment when life so easily converts to death.

The sun was going down, the temperature dropped instantly. Dick was on the verge of hypothermia and had a hard time making conversation; but he told Mario, "I'm so cold, we've got to get a fire going, a fire going." Mario replied, "I know Dick, I know. I'll find a place."

He saw some trees about 200 yards away, but didn't think they could make it. Dick was sizeably taller than his Italian friend, and his immense pain from one side of his shoulders to his thighs kept him from being able to stand. With every attempt to walk, he fell. Mario spotted a snag to the south of them, a distance he was in hopes that they could make. Dick said "Drag me. Drag me." "No Dick, no. You have to get up and help me or you will have hypothermia for sure. It's not far. You have to help me."

They struggled to get there. Inflicting more pain on Dick after what he had been through was miserable. Reaching that dead snag would be such a blessing if it had enough dry material to start the much-needed fire. The snag was, indeed, dry enough to serve the purpose.

Now, how to start a fire without their packs. Mario believes the good Lord was watching over them that day. He always keeps his matches in his backpack and NEVER carries a wallet. They both had their wallets that day, and Mario had matches in his pocket. He started with a blank check that he had. The fire began to consume the dry twigs, when a pile of snow dropped from the limbs above putting the fire out. Dollar bills began the next fire, Mario asked Dick if he had any money with him. Dick replied, shivering; "Yea, but don't burn that hundred dollar bill yet." Mario laughed, and knew at that moment that Dick was going to make it.

The fire began to take hold of the snag. The wind came up and gave the fire the air that it needed, so much so that the sparks and smoke became suffocating, but it was better than the cold. It became apparent that Dick was not recovering well. Mario said, "I'd better go for help." "No, don't go yet, don't go." Dick pleaded. Mario knew he had to do something, his heart was aching, as the anxiety of leaving Dick behind tore at the decision that he had to make. After a few more minutes, Dick reconsidered. "Yeah, maybe you had better go for help. I'm not feeling so good." Mario was relieved that the decision was made.

The fire was burning well and looked as if it would provide warmth for a few hours. Mario stuck Dick's ski about three feet from the edge of the snag and told him not to go past that ski. The snag would burn a hole and he didn't want Dick to fall in, which could easily happen if he fell asleep.

Mario began to walk down the mountain and got over the top of the Saddle and looked back. Dick was still standing there, holding onto the ski watching his friend walk away. Again, his heart agonized for having to leave Dick. Mario knew he had to get out of there as fast as he could. It took at least two hours to get down. Without the help of skis, he had to negotiate the deep snow on foot. Every step he took toward a tree well caused him to have to dig himself out of snow to his armpits. Even though the approaching dark and cold added to the misery, the reflection off of the bright, white snow make it easier to find his way.

Finally, the road where the truck was parked. A long-awaited relief, however, also agonizing that he had to waste time trying to get the truck turned around in the frozen snow. It seemed to take forever. He then thought to himself, "I will never leave a vehicle parked that is not ready to travel in the direction I am going." He went to the first house he came upon, and called the Sheriff, who got the Search and Rescue together.

By that time it was about 6:30 p.m. Mario still couldn't feel his exhaustion, the adrenalin still ran strong through his body, anxious for his fellow Search and Rescuers to arrive. He kept imagining Dick standing by the burning snag waiting for his return. Several men with snowmobiles finally arrived on the scene. They started back up the mountain where Mario had just come down hours before. The machines kept getting stuck, and became more trouble than help. Mario, an ambulance crew member named Norm, and Jim Heiland, a rescue member, decided to make the climb back up the mountain on foot. They grabbed a sleeping bag, coffee, food and radios. They began to hike the icy slope. They had hiked for just over two hours when Mario saw footprints coming down alongside his own that he left coming off the mountain. He said, "Do you think that could be Dick? Could he have decided that he could make it down?" By then, it was about 2:30 in the morning.

Within moments a rescue member called them on the radio from the camp they had set up with a large blazing fire. "He made it down, Mario. He's here." Mario replied in disbelief, "Would you repeat that?" "He's here. He's safe." Mario choked out his grateful reply, "That's the best present anyone ever gave me."

While Mario was going for help, Dick had begun to feel some of his strength return as the fire warmed him. The snag had burned a huge hole through the snow. He began to worry if Mario had made it down all right, it had been so long. He began to hike down using Mario's tracks to guide him off the mountain. There were moments that he regretted leaving the fire. Struggling through the deep snow and ignoring the stabs of pain seemed like a bad choice, until he saw the glow of the rescuer's fire, which gave him the encouragement he needed to finish his painful journey. He hadn't lost his sense of humor, for as he approached the camp through the dark shadows of the timber, he asked calmly, "Am I missing out on the party?" Everyone in camp looked as if they had seen a ghost. They ran to him in amazement. He received the warmest welcome he had ever known.

Mario almost ran down the mountainside after he heard the good news. He quickly left his companions behind, as his excitement replaced his fear and worry for his friend. By the time he made it to the camp, Dick had been taken to the hospital. Their time to share their multitude of feelings about the previous day's events would have to wait until later in the day. As Mario reached camp, Bob Cameron, another good friend who led the rescue effort, saw him and quickly strode toward him. The two men looked at each other in admiration and pride through their tears.

It was a time to be thankful for the miracle of a life-giving desire to overcome death that lives in each one of us. A victory that would stay with these avalanche survivors until it really is their time to leave these mysterious mountains.

Chapter 3

SEARCH AND RESCUE

I joined the Search and Rescue in 1973. About a year later we received a call toward the evening. A young man, in his twenties had lost his footing going up a steep section of a mountain and had tumbled about 100 feet down, coming to rest at a spot on the side of the mountain. This took place up near Big Creek Lake where three young men had been hiking together. One of the guys had rushed down to call the Sheriff while the other one had stayed with the injured man. Search and Rescue received the call and about a half dozen guys got under way to the scene. We waited at the base of the cliff where the injured man was, but we had to wait for daylight to get started up the cliff.

A fellow by the name of Bass was our leader as he had rock rescue experience. We climbed up to the injured man so we could bring him down. We set up ropes and attached the litter to it. We laid the man, who had a broken shoulder and broken ribs, in the litter and got ready to go down. One of the guys was in charge of carefully lowering the litter with a brake system. Bass, myself, and another fellow attached ourselves to the litter with slings and carabiners and all three of us had climbing belts on. Bass was at the foot of the litter and the other person and I were attached to the side. We slowly ascended. We soon came to the end of the rope, which was knotted at the end. We were now out of vision of the guy who was lowering us, and in those days we did not have any radios.

Bob Cameron, who was the Search and Rescue President at the time, was watching us from a distance. We needed to reset the ropes since we had to go further down to the bottom of the cliff. We secured the litter there. Since we could not communicate with the man up above to disconnect the rope, I told Bass I would disconnect my belt from the litter and free climb while holding onto the rope, until the upper man came into view. I was able to do this and told the man to wait about five minutes until I was back down at the litter and then to let the ropes go. Bob had seen what I did and told me later, "You are a mountain goat!" That's how I got my nickname, and from then on everyone in the Search and Rescue called me that.

We finally made it down to the valley floor. We had to carry the injured in the litter one-half mile on the trail to an open spot where the helicopter landed to pick him up. We hiked back down the canyon. A year later, Bass quit the Search and Rescue and I was elected to take over the rock climbing team. We often held practice sessions on the mountains.

The Rescue of Two Lost Hunters

On November 16, 1987, the Ravalli Search and Rescue received a call from the Sheriff's Department that two young men, Doyle and Steging, from the Malmstrom Air Force Base in Great Falls, had gone hunting near the end of Lost Horse Canyon and were overdue at their base camp. They had been last seen Friday the 13th of November, around 3:30 p.m., at the trailhead of Bailey Lake.

Around 6:30 p.m. we arrived at Lost Horse Cabin – Mark Kowack who was the head of the Hasty Team, myself, and other Search and Rescue members. That evening search efforts began. There was a few inches of snow on the ground.

The search lasted about over a week with more than 100 people involved, including personnel from the Air Base, a dog team, and aircraft, including a chopper from Malmstrom.

Mark Kowack and I were considered the toughest hikers in the Search and Rescue at the time. We decided on the third day of the search to scout a different area and walked past Bailey Lake over to the Idaho divide and down into the Granite Creek drainage for several miles. It was tough going as we were hiking through about two feet of snow. We had a radio with us and soon we realized it was a wasted effort because of all the snow.

We did not see any sign of the missing men, only animal tracks. Mark called Jerry Stewart, who was the president of the Search and Rescue at that time, who had set up a base at the cabin on the end of Lost Horse Canyon. A chopper from Malmstrom was parked near the cabin on stand-by and they used it to come down to Granite Creek and pick us up.

This helicopter was huge. We were standing pretty much in the center of the meadow so they could see us. The pilot radioed Mark and asked us to pack the snow down with our showshoes so he could land. About 20 minutes later we had it packed down as good as we could. Meanwhile, he was over us. We went into the trees while he came in for the landing. As he was coming close to the tree line, the big blades blew all the snow around in the area and we were concerned that the landing and takeoff would not go well. He made a safe landing, we hopped on board, and took off. As it was my first time in a helicopter, it was a little scary for me. We landed back at the cabin shortly thereafter. Other searchers kept looking for a few more days but then the search was canceled because of the heavy snow conditions.

The following year, in late June, Jerry Stewart suggested we pick up the search once more. Officials at the Malmstrom Air Force base wanted to help in locating the bodies. They sent about a dozen young men from the base to assist us. I took the Malmstrom group over the divide into Granite Creek Canyon. On the way down, we spread out, but we still could see each other so none of us would get lost. We kept looking for any sign until we reached the end of Granite Creek, then we turned into Bear Creek Canyon and ended up on the trail. It was slow going and some of the guys were getting pretty tired.

We were making a loop so we could get up to Lost Horse, the starting point. It made it more difficult because later on in the afternoon it started to rain and we were getting soaked. We finally made it back to the starting point at 1 a.m. the following morning. Mark Kowack, with the Hasty Team, had gone into Lost Horse Canyon to check the snow in late May and early June. While we were in the Granite Creek area searching, the Hasty Team and some other individuals were searching the same area of the year before. We all turned up empty.

In July, Art Griffith, who was an outfitter with a camp near Battle Lake, started to haul a load of supplies to his camp in order to get ready for the Fall season. He found Doyle's remains near Battle Creek Junction. He contacted Search and Rescue and a few individuals from the Team hiked to the spot where the body lay. The Idaho authorities arrived there before the Team and by the time they had arrived the body was scattered. In October, Griffith had hunters at his camp who stumbled onto the body of Steging in the Chute Creek area, near Battle Lake. They also found one of the rifles, and a scope which had been taken from another rifle which was never found.

The Missing Woman

A couple of years after the disappearance of Doyle Steging, I was involved with another search for a woman from Texas in the middle of September. This was in about the same area where they had found the bodies of the two airmen. The husband of the woman had acquired a hunting license to hunt in Montana, and had hired Art Griffith from Iron Horse Outfitters to guide him in his hunt. The wife had come along for the experience. She enjoyed taking picture and being in the wilderness.

Other hunters were also hunting with Iron Horse Outfitters. While the clients were out hunting, the lady stayed behind and visited with the cook who prepared the meals for the hunting crew. She asked for advice about going on a hike and wanted to know where it was safe and she could take some pictures. The cook suggested she might go down a trail below camp, which led to a large meadow, advising her that she might see some wildlife there.

The weather was nice and she made it down to the meadow where she had taken some pictures of a woodpecker pecking at a tree. Afterwards, she came back into camp. The following day she had decided to go back to the meadow again. The cook warned her not to get off the trail because she could easily get lost if she wandered off into the woods. She never came back to camp that day.

Since this was in Idaho, they called the authorities to help with the search. The sheriff in Idaho called the county sheriff in Hamilton, Montana, to get extra help from the Ravalli Search and Rescue. Jay Printz, who was the sheriff at that time, and Jerry Stewart, who was the President of Search and Rescue, assembled a crew consisting of Delbert Wood, Steve Clevidence, Dave Biddlecome and myself. We drove up Lost Horse Canyon and started hiking over Wahoo Pass into Idaho. The hike into the Iron Horse camp was over twenty miles. It took us all day to arrive at the camp. In the afternoon, it had started to rain and we were soaking wet.

The night after the woman had disappeared, the first skiff of snow had fallen and the weather had turned colder. We learned that she was not prepared for such conditions. She should have had a pack with her, some matches, warm clothing, and some food to snack on, but had none of these essential things.

The day after we got there, we went out searching the area for a while and came up empty.

We received word that the weather was going to change and that it was going to snow again. The Idaho authorities canceled the search, a decision I thought was stupid since we already had a bunch of searchers right there and the weather in September is still mild.

Garlick Helicopter Service out of Hamiltonwas hired to fly into the big meadow to pick up the Idaho authorities and bring them back to their stations. Ron Garlick, on the way back, landed again on the big meadow and picked up Dave Biddlecome and another person. Delbert Wood, Steve Clevidence and myself rode back on horses to the end of Lost Horse Canyon.

The missing woman had worked for the governor's office in Texas. The following summer, Texas authorities sent a helicopter with a search crew up, hoping to find the body but they were unsuccessful. Since this happened more than twenty years ago, my recollection of the events are a little foggy.

Plane Crash – 1991

The first week in October of 1991, we still had some fires here in Montana in the mountains. A plane was flown in from California to help with the fires, an old Army tanker plane piloted by First Officer Robert Shaw and Captain John Siglinger. They were getting ready to land at Missoula Airport late in the afternoon, but the weather had deteriorated and the plane ended up crashing on Little Joe Mountain, west of the small town of Stevensville.

The Search and Rescue teams from Ravalli and Missoula counties (of which I was a member at the time) were called in. By the time we arrived at the bottom of the mountain, it was dark. Since we did not know the exact location where the plane had gone down, we had to wait for the search until early the next morning.

The next morning I started hiking up Little Joe Mountain on the north side of Bass Creek when an individual approached me by the name of Mitch Cary and asked if he could go up with me. I said okay. Several other guys from the Ravalli Search and Rescue went up the south side of Bass Creek. As we were hiking up, a search plane was overhead and we were all in communication by radio and soon we were informed where the plane had gone down. We reached the location. It was a gruesome sight. The plane had hit the mountain about 300 yards from the top and pieces of the plane were scattered all the way up to the top. It had snowed three to four inches during the night. We were looking over the area when I found one of the bodies. The Missoula Search and Rescue had also arrived and they found the other body. I called the Ravalli Search and Rescue at the base of Little Joe, and told them what we had found. The sheriff, Jay Prince, showed up in a helicopter since he was also the coroner. We hiked back down while the bodies were retrieved.

A Happy Ending Rescue

On many occasions during the 20 years I was in the Search and Rescue we were called out on rescue missions. On one of these occasions, it involved two young college kids stuck on a cliff and they could not get off on their own. Bob Cameron, president of the Search and Rescue, and a few others and myself, received the call for help.

When we arrived at the site, I could see the young girl dangling at the end of a rope sixty feet short of the ground, and about fifteen feet away from the cliff. Apparently, she had been dangling there for about an hour. A young man wanted to come to her rescue and had down-climbed holding onto the rope, when he realized he could not help her or get himself back up on the cliff. Her sister, who was watching from the trail nearby, decided to drive over to Stevensville, a town a couple of miles away, and called the sheriff.

We rushed to the scene as fast as we could. Bob was wondering how we would get them out of their predicament, and I realized we had to do something pretty quick. I told Bob, "I think I'll free-climb to up alongside of her." In the meantime, Bob and another fellow hiked up the cliff hoping to see if they could help the boy up to the top of the cliff where he had tied his rope to a tree. They managed to throw a rope to the kid and then pulled him up. Bob and the other guy had brought an extra rope, pitons, and a hammer.

I made it up the cliff to a spot alongside the girl. One of the Search and Rescue members watched the progress from the trail. I told him to tell Bob that since I could not see him from where I was, to lower the spare rope he had, along with a bag of hardware. When the rope and bag got to me, I hammered a couple of pitons the cracks of the cliff, then clipped a couple of carabiners to the pitons and put the end of the rope through the carabiners. I could tell the girl was getting very tired holding on and told her I was going to throw the end of the rope to her and wanted her to catch it so I could pull her in. She caught the rope after a couple of tries. I said, "Hold on tight and I will pull you in." Then I pulled her to where I was.

I was also clipped into a carabiner and I tied the end of the rope which I was using to pull her with to her harness and slowly lowered her to the ground. It was a happy ending. Nobody was hurt. She later sent a postcard thanking me for saving her life.

Three close-up photographs of mountain lions taken by Mario on different trips into the mountains of western Montana.

Chapter 4

HIKING FOR CHARITY

Being part of the local Search and Rescue unit gave me a purpose. During a monthly meeting, discussion came up about raising some money for improving our old equipment as well as getting some new equipment. Group members were open for suggestions and I came up with the idea of organizing a race across the Bitterroot Mountains. Some of the group thought I was crazy and that it was too dangerous. I thought to myself, "These guys and gals don't know how determined I can be" and I set out to prove it could be done.

The money that was raised did not end up with the Search and Rescue organization because I did not get any more support from them. Lining up the race, I had to talk to the Forest Service because I was told that I needed a permit from them. We could not conduct any part of the race in the nearby Selway-Bitterroot Wilderness; under law, it had to be outside the boundaries of this legally-established wilderness. The only Bitterroot Valley canyon not in the wilderness proved to be Lost Horse Canyon and I asked Bill Goslin, a Forest Service employee, to accompany me on a hike to check out the area where I planned on having the race. We started out on Twin Lakes and straddled the wilderness boundary back to the end of Roaring Lion Road – an all-day hike.

I subsequently received a permit from the Forest Service to hold the race starting at Twin Lakes, which is at the end of Lost Horse Canyon, all the way to the end of Roaring Lion Road. There were three checkpoints along the mountain-tops; some friends from the Search and Rescue group stayed at the checkpoints and recorded the times of the participants on a checklist – requiring the participants to sign in at each of these checkpoints..

A group of endurance hike-a-thon participants atop El Capitan in the Bitterroot Range, Montana.

The races were held in July or early August, depending on how much snow was left on top of the mountains. Each of the participants had to meet with me before the race and had to hike to the checkpoints with me so they were aware of the terrain. This was done on three different Saturdays in June. I could then observe, and determine, if they had the qualifications to participate in the race. Over the years, I had from twenty-three to forty-four people in the race. Most of the them were from the local area, but a few came from such places as Washington state, California, Colorado and Oregon. Everyone was required to sign a waiver that they would not sue the Forest Service or me in case anyone would get hurt. The Forest Service insisted that I get insurance. They were always on my back about this, but no one wanted to provide any coverage; finally, however, I found an individual in Stevensville who came up with some insurance at a cost of $364 for a one-day event. This money could have gone to the event. After three years of races, I found out the insurance was not for the participants but only covered the spectators at the event. Anyhow, it did meet the requirements of the Forest Service! I then canceled the policy.

Mario captured this photograph of Jesse Bloom taking a picture of the whole group on one of the endurance hike-a-thon in the Bitterroot Range.

The fee per person for the race was $75 and everyone would get a T-shirt on which the event's name was printed with a mountain goat logo in the background; John Germann always made a sizeable donation toward meeting this cost of the race. Every year the price of the entry fee was raised a little. The charity that the money was raised for that year would be printed on the T-shirt. Usually between $2,000 and $3,000 would be raised at each event.

Some people would not race, but just walk the course. I would bring up the rear of the crowd for safety reasons, beginning at 6:00 a.m., and be in communication via my walkie-talkie with the checkpoints. Since I was with the slower group for safety precautions, we would sometimes not get to the end until 1:00 a.m. the following morning. Even just walking over the route, with some eighty percent of it being across rock slides, finishing the course was quite an accomplishment.

The second year of the mountain goat run, I decided to participate in my own race and had Jim Martin bring up the rear for me. To my total surprise, I won my own race! I did the course of about twenty-five miles in seven hours and forty minutes. The next person behind me came in fifty-five minutes later.

Every year we had some who would not finish the entire course because their legs would give out. They would head down to Lost Horse Road, and someone who would be driving the road would pick them up. Again, the Forest Service was giving me a hard time since I did not have the liability insurance; so, after five years, I quit the races and started having an Endurance Hike over the Bitterroot Mountains.

The participants and I would hike around twenty-five to thirty miles in one day. Still the Forest Service was complaining. A couple of employees from the Forest Service wanted me to get together with them to find a solution to the problem: they informed me that I could not have people hiking with me as long as I did not have liability insurance – in spite of me telling them that the money was not for me but for charity and that no one would insure us.

Mario taking a break on one of the endurance hikes.

I then suggested to start a Mountain Goat Club and charge a fee to join, but I could not advertise in the paper what the fee would be. When someone would call me to participate in a hike I would then let them know how much it was. That's how I got around the problem. We usually had around twenty to thirty hikers. We did this for several years until the Forest Service, again, got on my back over the insurance issue. By that time I was getting burned out and after eleven years of races and hikes I called it quits.

I had a good group of people helping me with the events and

without their support it would have never happened, and they deserve a big thank you. Among those in the crew that helped with the races were: Les Rutledge, Jerry Lewis, Delbert Wood, Jerry Swanson, Billy Jamerson, Joe Bender, John Germann, Jerry Stewart, Marill and son Matt, Shellee Abel, Art Howard and son Dave, Charles and Ruth Center, Jerry Milligan, Allen McClintick, and Mary McClintick. I also appreciated help from two local grocery stores, IGA and Super One in Hamilton, for donating the refreshments for the events. Several local restaurants donated vouchers for meals and prizes and my brother's restaurant, "A Hole in the Wall" in Las Vegas, Nevada, plus Horst Dziura, President of the Hilton Hotel in Las Vegas at that time, supported the race. The vouchers and prizes were handed out on a first-come, first-serve basis, as the participants reached the end of the line, until we ran out.

- 1989, Lifeline/Marcus Daly Memorial Hospital – $1,075.00
- 1990, United Veterans Council – $2,014.55
- 1991, United Veterans Council – $2,059.63
- 1992, The Todd Family – $2,170.00
- 1993, St. Patrick Hospital Life Flight – $3,163.00
- 1994, Karlins Family – $2,250.00
- 1995, Don Mackey Memorial – $1,860.00
- 1996, St. Patrick Hospital Life Flight – $3,000.00
- 1997, Disabled American Veterans Van – $2,000.00
- 1998, Corvallis Library – $2,150.00
- 1999, St. Patrick House – $2,000.00
   Corvallis Woodside Bike Path – $730.00
- 2000, Sam Keskeny (burn victim) – $2,400.00
- 2006, Firefighter Memorial – $2,467.21

Total of $29,339.39

My daughter, Cathy, "carrying" me on one of our hikes in the Bitterroot Mountains.

Chapter 5

THE BITTERROOT – RIVERS AND MOUNTAINS

When I first moved into the Bitterroot Valley, my TV quit working one evening and, after looking in the telephone book trying to find someone to fix TV's, I called Rick Klin. He came to the house and fixed the TV. Since he had been living in the Bitterroot for a few years already, we visited about all the outdoor activities and recreational hobbies he had. I thought this guy was right up my alley; we seemed to enjoy the same things. This was at the end of May in 1973 when we met, and the Bitterroot River was running high that spring. He told me that some of his friends were planning to float the river and he asked me if I wanted to go along.

We started out at Angler's Roost just south of Hamilton. Rick and one of his buddies were going in kayak, and the other friend and I were in a small aluminum boat. Rick had a wetsuit on, the other two were dressed more appropriately for the outing than I was. I was the rookie of the four and had never floated on a river before, except in the big boat coming over from Italy. I was wearing a brand new pair of cowboy boots, jeans, and had topped it off with a straw hat – all of which were definitely the wrong things to wear.

At first it was a little scary for me, but after a little while I thought it was not so bad and, actually, sort of fun. We made it to West Main Bridge in Hamilton; I could see an obstruction ahead of us. The farmers, at one time, had put a rough wall across the river so they could divert the water into a big ditch for irrigating. We could not stop the boats and had to go with the flow.

We finally went over the rock wall and dropped down about ten feet. As soon as we plunged over the wall, the boat slid to one side and we landed in the water. Apparently, the kayak was more stable and made it over the wall without a problem. We hung onto the side of the boat. I struggled but finally managed to pull myself inside. The other guy was trying to get back in also. He was heavier than I was and he ended up flipping me back into the water and he did not make it back into the boat.

Mario jokingly does one of his traditional head-stands on the limb of an old tree during a climb of Little Downing Mountain in the Bitterroot Range.

    I lost my hat. I realized this was a hopeless situation and thought about swimming back to shore. As I was swimming toward shore, I began getting tired right off the bat – my boots were full of water. I pulled them off and let them go. I realized the water was moving very fast and it was very cold. It made sense to me that I had to change my strategy. I floated with the current and began guiding myself gradually toward the shore. I could see up ahead where a tree stump with the roots sticking into the river. I managed to reach the stump and grab one of the roots. I held on for dear life! I then managed to hoist myself onto shore.

    This floating trip ended for me right then and there, and this adventure could have actually gotten me killed. The rest of the crew decided to continue down the river. They ended up slamming into a log jam further down. They survived but it got a little hairy, they told me later. After I had joined the Search and Rescue, several individuals drowned on this river. On one occasion a person had slammed into a tree with their kayak, and the kayak wrapped itself right around the tree.

During the spring when the water is high, these rivers can be extremely dangerous; so be aware.

Rick and I stayed in touch and went on several hikes together. He was ten years younger than I and he was a vegetarian. On my first hike with him, I wondered what kind of hiker he was, since I consider myself to be in pretty good hiking shape. Going up the mountain we were pretty much equal, but coming down I had a hard time keeping up with him since he was about seven inches taller than I.

On one trip in the winter, we decided to climb El Capitan, which is the second tallest mountain in the Bitterroot Valley. We started out at Little Rock Creek. By the time we had reached the base of El Capitan, the weather turned kind of nasty and we thought it best to stay there and wait. We dug a trench and put a tarp over it for sleeping. We spent three nights at this spot.

Around us were a few standing dead trees, so I climbed up and broke some dry branches off so we could make a fire and cook some food. We each had a little pot, melted some snow in it for water, and as soon as it boiled we cooked some Ramen noodle soup. We snacked on cheese and salami, and for dessert had candy bars. On the third day, we were running out of food and we decided to try and make it to the top as the weather had improved a little. We had to hike up through a very steep coulee that led to the top.

Mario atop an old cabin on Little Joe west of Stevensville

One of the routes taken on a hike-a-thon. Dusty Woods watches as Mario climbs before the rest of the crew followed.

Even though we were wearing snowshoes, we could not go straight up but had to zig-zag back of forth. Both of us were pretty green and could have easily started an avalanche in this area. We managed to reach the top in about three hours. It was very windy and cold on the peak. We snapped a few pictures and then headed down. We made it out of there to our vehicles the same day. We actually did not even have the proper clothing for such an outing – wearing jeans and cotton shirts. The only good thing I had was my down sleeping bag, which I had stuffed down into a feed sack and tied to my back. The both of us took many more trips together. He was quite a daredevil. I thought a few times, "I better be careful; this guy is going to get me killed."

During the winter, Rick would ride on chunks of ice down the Bitterroot River. I liked Rick a lot. He never had a negative thing to say about anybody. He was a very spiritual person and he had a good sense of humor. He has two boys and moved to Libby, Montana, twenty-five years ago. Occasionally, I talk to him on the phone and we will reminisce about the 'good ole days'.

Another good friend by the name of Leon Anderson and I did quite a few hikes together. He and his family moved to Colville, Washington, about twenty years ago so they could be near her father and mother. Dusty Wood, who has been like the son to me that I never had, climbed a few mountains with me. We also did some more climbing and alpine skiing together. John Klingbeil was another friend who often came with us on climbs and alpine skiing. John was a natural when it came to rock climbing. Here is a list of names of all the friends and acquaintances who accompanied me on hikes, rock climbing, and alpine skiing. I apologize if I inadvertently left anyone out:

Garry Hall	George Looker	Joe and Nancy Bender
George Corn	Steve Powell	Bob Brophy
Skip Horner	Thomas Evans	Allen Thompson
Scott Lebinguth	Batista Locatelli	Howard Anderson
Paul Begins	John Perry	Will Wilkinson
Michael Brooke	Delbert Wood	Dick Robinson
Mark Kowack	Jim and Jason Kacbier	Bill Goslin
Vic Raso	Tanya and Jesse Seth Bloom	Jeremy Lurgio
Steward Donaldson	John German	Kathy Locatelli
Carmela Locatelli	Jerry Swanson	Dean Lanfort
Ed Pine	Bob Wentz	Mark Waltenski
Chris Devine	Pete Locatelli	Vitorio Locatelli
Allen and Jesse Applebury		

Cathy and Mario on Trapper Peak in the Bitterroot Range.

Chapter 6

A WALK WITH MARIO
(Told by Cathy Locatelli)

We've all heard the expression, "It's never too late". Seventy-year-old Mario Locatelli is bagging the most impressive summits of the Lower 48, each in one day, while setting impressive pace times. Upon reaching each pinnacle, he goes into his victory headstand as if to offer his unfailing feet to the heavens in gratitude for conquering another peak, adding it to his encouraging list of achievements. He is truly a man of great motivation and inspiration to others of all ages. His step never seems to slow – each year more precise and determined. "Let's mosey," he'll say, one rocky brush-filled mile after another, following only the contour of the land. I know him well; his encouragement over the years motivates me to hike farther, higher, in the dark, in the cold, lifting my spirits, lightening my burdens, strengthening my character.

Born December 21, 1932, on the first day of Winter in Berbenno, Italy, third in a line of twelve siblings, he was cast aside by other children in such sports as soccer because of his small frame, and subjected to cruel names. Driven by rejection, he began to hike the nearby hills searching for seclusion. He loved the feeling elevation gave him, so he began to climb the church steeple – reaching the needle and proving to himself that his size was not a limitation. "I was like a spider. I could climb anything. I found out something that I could do better than the other kids."

Sixteen years old and weighing eighty-eight pounds, he traveled to the United States with a sister, one brother, and two cousins. It took eleven days on a ship named "Vulcania" to New York, followed by four days by train to Oakland, California, and then to Santa Cruz by car. He ate only one meal and completed the trip with no money. They worked in the fields for menial pay until they could find their way into better jobs, always stepping up into laboring positions that were meant for larger men.

Mario said: "When I turned 18, my cousins and I wanted to work in a quarry. The owners didn't want to hire us because they thought we weren't big and heavy enough, although I had grown to 135 pounds. They wanted us to be at least 150 pounds to handle a 90-pound jackhammer. Lucky for us the employees went on strike. In those days the boss said come to work or lose your job. We got the jobs and about killed ourselves to prove we could do as good or better than the bigger guys. We were drilling 21 feet into limestone. I'd put my leg over the top of the jackhammer handle to accelerate the drilling rate. One day the drill bit snapped and nicked the edge of my toe. I didn't tell anyone. When I got home afterward, I took my boot off and discovered it was full of blood. I continued to work afterward because I didn't want to lose the job. The boss was so impressed with our performance, they changed their policy and hired men under 150 pounds."

Mario married and had four daughters. At age thirty-five, he moved to Oregon and became a demolition contractor. "I wanted to be closer to the mountains. In Italy, I lived in the mountains and worked in the mountains and never lost my desire for altitude," he said.

In 1967, Mario made plans to satisfy his craving to climb a "big" mountain, the highest summit in Oregon. Climbing Mount Hood involves a six-mile hike to 11,239 feet, a 5,319-foot elevation gain. Equipped with crampons and an ice ax, he and seventeen-year-old friend Gary Wall started from the Timberline Lodge at 5:00 a.m. Less than 300 yards from the top, they caught up with a small group of climbers who were roped up, equipped with hard hats, crampons, ice axes and weather-resistant clothing. The well-equipped group had started from the Lodge at 1:00 a.m., everyone reaching the summit at approximately 10:55 a.m. One of the climbers commented to Mario and Gary, "You guys must have climbed a bunch of mountains; you're really good!". It was then that Mario realized he might have a gift. On the way down the mountain, he ran fearlessly. His companion slipped and started rolling and pitching down the mountain. Mario ran ahead of him, breaking his fall before he was badly injured. It was not until then that he realized the dangerous and possibly fatal consequences. They completed their climb in just less than ten hours, reaching the Lodge by 3:00 p.m. the same day.

He moved to Montana five years later. He was forty years old and going through a divorce. He began going to the local saloons and feeling like he was dying inside. Determined to feel better, he put on his hiking boots and headed into the Bitterroot Selway – the largest section of wilderness in the Lower 48. And it was right out his back door! At least once a week he would start out with a full pack, walk to the end of a canyon by the Montana-Idaho border, which averaged from ten to thirteen miles long, climb one of the canyon walls to the ridge and hike back home – a round trip which took around thirteen to fourteen hours. He would drop back down into the drainage and mark his spot until he could return another day to complete the ridge he started. He told me, "I got over my divorce and began to feel like a soaring eagle."

It took Mario twenty years to finish his goal – thirty-nine canyons and approximately 2,400 miles of mostly granite slides. He became agile and fast in the rock. When asked how he does it, he says, "I just kiss 'em and leave 'em." Boulders can range from the size of a football to that of a semi truck.

He served in the Search and Rescue for twenty years, during which time he was head of the Rock Climbing Team for twelve years, experiencing himself in mountaineering and avalanche courses. The training came in handy when he and Dick Robertson were caught in a slab avalanche on February 28, 1981. The estimated speed of the slide was sixty miles an hour. Back country skiing at the time, the fracture broke above Dick as they were crossing a chute. Mario was able to keep on top of it; however, his friend was buried except for a two-inch patch of his pants that was visible. Mario was able to dig his friend out before he suffocated. They started a small fire with the paper money they had. Mario knew Dick was going to be all right when Dick said "Don't burn that hundred dollar bill yet!"

Mario organized a fund-raising hike, suitably named the "Mountain Goat Marathon" that gave funds to organizations such as Life Flight and various catastrophes. The route covered twenty-five miles across the rugged wall of the Bitterroot Selway, beginning at Twin Lakes which is on the edge of the Montana-Idaho border. The hike involved various elevations from 6,500 feet, up and down across the canyon walls to the tallest summit of Ward Mountain (9,119 feet). There were three checkpoints where each hiker had to sign off. It was approximately 80 percent rock, without trails, except the last mile out. At the age of fifty-seven, Mario won his own race in seven hours and forty minutes. The record for the route was set by thirty-six-year-old Scott Leibenguth –

six hours and 59 minutes. After six years, the race was converted to Endurance Hikes, since the Forest Service required liability insurance that was cost prohibitive to the race. The "Mountain Goat Club" was born and evolved into twenty-five to thirty-mile endurance hikes, and founder Mario Locatelli was nicknamed the "Mountain Goat". The Forest Service continued to hamper the race due to liability issues, so after a total of twelve years and $28,000 of funds raised for good causes, the hikes ended. It was then that Mario began hiking and climbing the highest peaks in each state, asking a friend or two to go with him, beginning with Mount Rainier in Washington State. Equipped with day packs, food, warm clothes, an ice ax, crampons and one sixty-feet eleven-mm rope, they completed the climb from the bottom to the top and back in sixteen hours. He subsequently stated, "If I had it to do over again, I would have used a 9 mm rope, it's lighter."

Granite Peak, 12,799 feet high and the highest mountain in Montana, was his next accomplishment on August 31, 1996. A twenty-three-mile round trip done in eighteen hours. Then, at sixty-three years of age, Mario reached the summit without a partner, equipped with only one ski pole. Between the summer of 1997 and mid-2004, Mario reached the summit of the highest mountains in the United States, with the exception of Mount McKinley in Alaska. Mario said, "I want to do McKinley. I know I am fit enough but the expense and knowing I may have to wait out the weather for days, makes me apprehensive. I can't take the cold like I used to."

Other peaks that Mario completed in one day, traveling light and equipped with only a ski pole and crampons are:
- Mount Shasta – 14,162' – top to bottom in 15½ hours
- Mount Whitney, California – 14,494', a 21½ mile hike done in 11½ hours.
- Mount Adams, Washington – 12,307', 11 hours.
- Mount Borah, Idaho – 12,552', 6½ miles in 5 hours and 50 minutes.
- Mount Elbert, Colorado – 14,433', a nine-mile hike in 5 hours and 5 minutes.
- Gannett Peak, Wyoming – 13,804', a 15-mile hike starting where Tourist Creek merges with Green River, completed in 14½ hours.
- Humphrey's Peak, Arizona – 12,633', a nine-mile hike in 4 hours and 15 minutes.
- Kings Peak, Utah - 13,528' – 28 miles in 13 hours.

- Boundary Peak, Nevada – a six-mile hike in 4 hours and 50 minutes.
- Devil's Tower, Wyoming – 875' of rock, done in 6 hours.
- McDonald Peak, Montana – done in 11½ hours.
- Guadeloupe Peak, Texas – done in 3 hours and 15 minutes.
- He was weathered out on Wheeler Peak in New Mexico.
- Mount Saint Helens – 8,300', done totally on skis in 9 hours, up and back. He says with a chuckle, "St. Helen's used to be higher but the top got blown off!"

Mario has kept his weight at 145 pounds for the past forty years. He stays in shape through climbing the Bitterroot peaks in winter using back county skis and snowshoes, and tracks mountain lions. He never experiences altitude sickness, just loss of appetite. "This is my time," he says, "I don't know how much time I have left but I feel good and have many more peaks ahead of me. If I had started younger, I would have tried Mount Everest. I need to keep doing it; it keeps me charged up. I don't want people to think these climbs were done unprepared. Doing a mountain in one day, you have to stay alert and be ready to get off the mountain fast. I did not make all of these peaks the first time."

Mario is a member of the High Pointers Club, based in Golden, Colorado, with more than 2,500 members. He hopes to hike all the highest peaks in the Lower 48.

Mario said he would like to thank Dusty Wood, Bill Goslin and John Klingbil for accompanying him when they could.

An Italian boy – driven by high goals and distant dreams. A man – living the balance of his life without limitations, full of challenge and adventure, appreciating his freedom.

"Let's mosey...."

Mario captured this picture of one of his neighbors, a Downey woodpecker, in its nest along Mario's fence-line at his home in the Bitterroot Valley in western Montana.

Chapter 7

HUNTING IN THE BITTERROOT

One of my greatest passions was being outdoors hunting and fishing. My love for hunting started in California. I moved to Montana to the Bitterroot Valley for the beauty of the area and the opportunity for me to hunt every species there was around. I went after moose, bighorn sheep, whitetail and mule deer, mountain goat, bear, antelope and mountain lion, as well as birds. For my mountain lion hunting I owned several good Bluetick hounds and I did that mostly on foot. I treed quite a few lions with my hounds, but for most of them I only took pictures of and then let them go. I have taken a few lions with my longbow. I also have taken a couple of mountain goats with my longbow, but most of the time I hunted with my .257 Weatherby rifle.

The last thirty years I have limited my hunting to several of the canyons on the west side of the Bitterroot Valley, with my favorite going up Sawtooth Canyon. It was very remote and not that easy to get into, but I enjoyed it the most. I had my own horses and mules. In the fall I would make a half dozen trips up there to hunt for elk and mule deer. Most of the time, I was by myself and would stay out for about four days. After a few days, I would miss my family and go home for a few days, then I would head back out again.

At the end of August, I would go into Sawtooth and set up my 12x14 wall tent with a wood stove. It was about two miles from the Idaho border right on the valley floor and below Ingomar Lake, right alongside Sawtooth Creek, where I would set up my camp. I had some great times up there. I passed up many, many mule deer looking just for the right big buck. I used to get a bull elk up there every year, and as long as a bull was legal I would take him. I bagged several six-point bulls and have taken a few with my longbow. My family and I enjoyed the meat and gave away some of the meat to friends because we had more than we needed. I also have taken six bears with the longbow, and two with a rifle. We ate some of the bear meat as well as the lion meat. The hides I had tanned and gave a few away to my relatives in Italy and I also sold some.

Fishing at Ingomar Lake resulted in some dandy fish – from twelve to twenty inch trout – and they were very good eating because the water is cold at 7,000 feet elevation. Some days you could catch them very easily, and other days they just would not bite. I mostly just caught enough for me to eat while I was camping there. I very seldom took any home. On days I could not catch any from the lake, I would fish the stream and catch eight to ten-inch brookies, enough to make a meal. After they were fried in a heavy-duty cast iron frying pan, I would squeeze some lemon juice on them. Boy, were they ever good!

Usually when I was at my hunting camp, I would block off the trail by laying some logs across it, and then I would turn the horses loose. This prevented them from going home. Close by was a nice meadow with lots of grass where the animals would graze. I did that for several years, then the horses got smart and started going further up the canyon where I would have to look for them. I started to tie up a few of the animals on a high-line and the rest of them I let go so they could graze. I would rotate them. I always had some oats or pellets along and would feed them a little of that.

On one hunting trip I came back to camp about noon. I had a gelding and a mule tied on the high-line with another gelding loose grazing when, all of a sudden, a very strong gust of wind came up – trees were blowing over and I was very concerned that my animals and I would get hit! Suddenly, I could see one tree very close to me falling right toward me. I ran off to the side to get away but the top of the tree hit the mule in the head. It scratched him up some, but was not serious. The wind lasted only a few minutes and then stopped. I then looked for the loose gelding and saw my horse laying next to a tree which had come down. I thought he might just be knocked out. I couldn't believe what I saw! It appeared he had gotten hit in the head. He was such a gentle and fine animal. I took it very hard since I was very attached to my animals. I got emotional and started to cry. I ended up having to leave the carcass there.

Mario climbing in Blodgett Canyon with Dusty Wood.

Mario with his oldest daughter, Cathy, on Gash Peak in the Bitterroot Range.

1995 hike in the Bitterroot Mountains of western Montana.

A group photo of an endurance hike on top of El Capitan, the second highest peak in the Bitterroot Mountains in southwestern Montana.

Atop Granite Peak in Montana. From left are Bob Wentz, Dusty Wood, John Klingbeil and Mario.

A break taken at Duffy Lake on one of our benefit hike-a-thons.

Mario does his head-stand on top of Devil's Tower in Wyoming.

Climbing Devil's Tower in Wyoming in 2000 with Dusty Wood and Dave Biere.

Climbing Mount Hood in Oregon.

The "first" picture of one of Mario's triumphant head-stands, taken atop McDonald Peak in the Mission Mountains.

Mario on the top of Trapper Peak in the Bitterroot Mountains of western Montana.

Mario on top of Gannett Peak in Wyoming.

Mario on top of Guadalupe Peak, the highest in Texas.

Mario on Mount Adams in Washington state, with Mount Ranier in the background.

Mario at Boulder Point near the West Fork of the Bitterroot River in western Montana.

Ice on Kilimanjaro in Africa.

Mario with Dusty Wood and John Perry on top of Borah Peak, the highest in Idaho.

Mario doing his head-stand on Gannett Peak, the highest in Wyoming.

Mario with David Biere and Dusty Woods atop Devil's Tower in Wyoming.

Mario on Trapper's Peak in the Bitterroot Range in western Montana.

Mario with Dusty Wood (center) and Bill Goslin on top of McDonald Peak in the Mission Mountains in Montana.

Mario on top of Mount Hood in Oregon.

Mario does his head-stand on to of Mount Shasta in California, June 12, 1998.

Mario performing the head-stand on top of Mount St. Helen in Washington state, with Mount Rainier in the background.

Mike Brooke, Joe Bender and Mario on one of the Benefit Hike-a-thons held in the Bitterroot Mountains.

Mario on top of Mount Whitney, the highest peak in California.

Mario on top of Wheeler Peak in New Mexico.

Mario does his traditional head-stand on top of Granite Peak, the highest in Montana.

Mario waves an American and Italian flag on top of Mount McKinley in Alaska.

Mario does his head-stand on Mount McKinley in Alaska under the watchful eye of his guide, Zach Shloson.

Doing a traverse across a canyon in Mill Creek, Bitterroot Range, with Dusty Wood and several other members of the Search and Rescue unit.

Mario with his wife, Liesa, on Mount Mauna Kia on the Big Island, Hawaii.

For five or six years, my brother, Baptista, and Horst Dziure would come from Las Vegas to hunt with me. During that period, they had no problems getting a license to hunt in Montana. Later the Fish and Game Department changed the regulations and it became more difficult to get a license. Once in a while, I would take a few close friends up to my camp to hunt with me. When I was alone, I only took three animals, but when I was with a hunting party I would take all my animals – five of them.

Around 1975 I met Dick Robertson, who was quite an outdoorsman and one of the best bowhunters in the Valley. I learned a lot from him about how to hunt with a bow. He had started making longbows and made a couple for me. He became a very good bowmaker and ended up shipping them all over the world.

The sun peaking through the clouds on Mount Rainier in Washington state.

Chapter 8

KEEPING THE MOUNTAINS CLEAN

It was 1976, the first year I started hunting and fishing in Sawtooth Canyon, when I noticed a shiny object on the skyline near the Montana-Idaho border. I decided to investigate and hiked up. When I got there, I could see a wrecked plane. It must have hit pretty hard because the twin engines were laying about 100 feet apart from each other. I was in the Search and Rescue at the time, and Dale Dye was the sheriff at that time. I went to see him after I returned from my hike. I asked him if he knew about the plane crash and when and how it occurred. He filled me in on the details.

A fellow by the name of Larry Larson from Mountain Home, Idaho, fell asleep and crashed a couple hundred of feet below the Montana-Idaho divide. Dale Dye and one of his deputies, by the name of Alan Horsfall, had been flown to the site by a helicopter to investigate but were not able to land at the spot, so they landed a little lower than the crash site. They hiked up with a litter; the body was laying on a big boulder and they brought him down. The pilot of the chopper was Wayne Miller. The plane had caught fire on impact.

I then went to the Forest Service in Hamilton and talked to the people in charge of removing the wreckage. They kept telling me some day...some day – empty promises – and it frustrated me greatly. One day, I called the Forest Service office in Darby and talked to Tom Wagner, the head of the office. I got immediate results by talking to him – a very super-nice man. He suggested that I find someone to go up with me and gather all the small pieces and bag them up. I called my friend, Bill Goslin, the wilderness ranger from Stevensville. We had done some hiking and alpine skiing together. He agreed to go up with me. He said he had a friend in Missoula by the name of John DeVore and that he would also come along.

Bill called the Back Country Horsemen – a organization that does a lot of volunteer work cleaning up trails in the back country – my hat is off to them! Some of the members helped us pack in. I had a lot of feed sacks that I had saved. We packed our supplies up by Blodgett Lake, which had quite a nice trail. The crash site was about one a half miles over the hill from there. Sawtooth Canyon is very hard to get into with horses. Bill, John and I hiked up to the lake where we set up camp and spent the night there before we would set out on our task.

Early the next morning, we hiked up to the crash site and sacked up about twenty sacks of small pieces of metal and plastic, etc. We put the sacks all in a pile. It took most of the day to get the job done, then we hiked back home. The following day, the men that had brought our supplies up came back up to get our personal stuff. I called Tom Wagner and told him everything was ready to be picked up. He told me he had a chopper on stand-by to pick up the wreckage. I asked if I could ride along in the chopper, but it was against regulations and they could not allow it.

He wanted me to be at the crash site when the chopper arrived and he was sending a man by the name of Marty, who worked for the Forest Service, to help me put the stuff in the net. I rode my gelding and packed one of my mules up Sawtooth to my hunting camp, where I stayed overnight. I hiked up there and just as I arrived, the chopper showed up. He dropped Marty off and then lowered the net on a long cable. As the chopper hovered, we hurried to put the sacks in the net. He dropped a few chokers down to us and then hauled the sacks to the valley floor. A semi was waiting to have the wreckage loaded. While he was gone, we put the chokers on the two engines, which were estimated to weigh 400 pounds each. He made a couple more trips back and forth and picked up all the other pieces. By 2:00 pm, we were done. I took pictures of the chopper as it was lifting everything and flew off. I told Tom Wagner how grateful I was that the place was cleaned up. A few years later when talking to Bill Goslin, I found out that Marty had been caught in a avalanche and had perished.

On one of my hikes when I climbed up to a high ridge halfway between Ward Mountain and the Idaho border I discovered eight rusted-out five-gallon milk cans. I also found a couple of pulaski, which is a tool used in fire-fighting or when working on clearing trails on the mountains, lunch boxes, and some other debris. One of the milk cans had a tag tied on the lid which said "Poison" on it. When I got back home, I called the Darby Forest Service office and described what I had found. I asked them if they would send some Forest Service people up with me so we could go and clean up the mess and bring everything down.

When I asked them if they knew about that stuff, they said no. They also said they did not have anyone available who could go up there. I then called Allen Thompson, a friend, and asked him if he would like to go with me and help bring the stuff down. He agreed.

We met early one morning and he brought one of his sons, Eric, along also. We hiked to the place where all the junk was laying around. We each had brought a pack frame along to tie the cans onto. The cans weighed about twenty-five pounds each, so we only could pack one can apiece and Eric took the lids. Before we strapped the cans onto the pack frame, we stacked all eight cans, with four on each side, and took a picture so we would have proof of the mess up there. When we got home, I had the picture developed and went to see the Ravalli newspaper.

I gave them the picture and also the tag which said "Poison" on it. Meanwhile, I had also found out that the cans were hauled up there by the Forest Service up to the top of the ridge with spray in them by a helicopter to spray for beetle bugs. The newspaper published what I had reported. I received a call from the head of the Forest Service in Darby, and he was very upset that I had done that. I figured I finally got some attention with regard to this matter. Suddenly, the Forest Service had five young men available. We all hiked up to the place and packed everything down, which took us all day. The Forest Service let me keep two of the cans that I had found.

Mario with a bear he took with the longbow.

Chapter 9

BEARS

During my hunting trips up Sawtooth Canyon in the Bitterroot Mountains near my home, I had problems with bears on several occasions. One time, I had shot a bull elk in the morning, gutted it out and then quartered it. By the time I got back to camp with the meat, it was getting dark so I laid the quarters on some small logs so the meat would air out overnight.

I would usually take a long pole (small tree) and tie it with ropes between two trees about 12 feet apart and about 12 feet off of the ground. I would then throw a rope over the pole and pull up each quarter, tying them off to nearby trees. This would keep the bears from getting to the elk quarters. However, when I woke up the next morning, I had my breakfast and, when I stepped out of my tent to take care of the meat, I discovered one of the hind quarters was missing.

I could see where a bear had come during the night; he had left a trail from dragging the meat away. I followed the evidence about 100 yards and saw the missing piece laying in the woods. Evidently, this was a very neat bear – he only ate about two to three pounds of flesh from the hind quarter's choice meat. I guessed that he might have heard me coming and took off, spoiling his meal. I then dragged the meat back to camp and then hung it over the pole and decided to change my plans for the day: I had planned to go fishing at nearby Ingomar Lake, but decided it was best to take the elk meat home, so I loaded it on my animals and took it out.

Several times over the years the bears have vandalized my tent looking for food. When I had left-over food, I would tie it up in the trees where it would be safe until I returned to my camp. Once I came back to the tent and I found my goods were sitting on the ground. The bear had managed to get into the goodies; even the canned food had holes punched into them where it had tried to get to the inside! After that, I brought the left-over food back to the house.

On another occasion I took a friend with me. He had never killed a bear and wanted me to help him get one. On that trip I had killed a bull elk. We hauled the meat up and to entice the bear I cut a neck piece and let it hang low enough for the bear to reach. Early the next morning, just as it was getting daylight, two of my mules which were tied to a tie-line not far from where the meat was hanging were getting nervous. I could hear them stomping, so I told my friend that there was a bear outside and to get his gun ready. It was now full daylight so he could see the bear clearly and, as soon as I opened the tent flap, I yelled at him to get out and let him have it. Sure enough, he shot him and got himself a very nice bear.

On a different hunting trip I had another friend with me and we had our elk meat hanging on the pole when, early in the morning, we heard a commotion outside. This friend had a bear tag and he asked me if I would mind if he shot it. Sure enough, outside was a nice cinnamon-colored black bear. As soon as he saw it, he tried getting away but my friend nailed him. He turned out to be six feet long.

When I was sleeping in my tent, I would dream the bears were coming after me. I would catch myself waking up yelling and I've always been happy that each time it turned out to be just a dream.

Chapter 10

PACK ANIMALS – MULES AND HORSES

During the hunting I did over the years, I raised a few good mules. The mules take a lot of patience when you train them, and they are a lot smarter than horses, and are better in the mountains than horses, especially for packing.

You have to work with mules constantly when they are young, but once they realize that you won't hurt them, they accept you and trust you and will give you back loyalty and follow you anywhere

I also owned a few good geldings, but since they lacked mountain experience, I had to train them for this kind of work. My first gelding was a four-year-old Quarterhorse named Dodger, but I renamed him Chief because I did not like the name Dodger. The lady I bought him from had trained him so that as soon as you got on him, he started to run. When I started using him to go into the mountains, I would pull the reins a little and call out, "Easy, easy." He finally gave up his bad habit and I would lead my mules behind him. Chief had a good disposition and after being up and down the mountains with him a couple of years, he turned out to be a heck of a mountain horse. I had him for about eighteen years.

Any time I would get an elk alongside a steep mountain, I would take Chief with me. I would put a pack saddle on him and zig-zag him through the trees to the spot where the elk laid. When I would reach the spot, I would stand the horse just a few feet below the elk and he would just stand there patiently while I loaded one piece of the meat on him. Then I would turn the horse around and do the same with another piece of meat. It would take two trips – the first trip I would pick up the hind quarters, and the second trip I would haul down the front pieces. I would take my time when leading him back to camp. It was fun working with Chief. It eventually got to the point where it was too hard for him to go up into the mountains with me, even though he was willing.

I saw in the paper where a rancher was looking for a gentle, older horse that his young daughter could ride, and I sold Chief to the rancher. I then bought another gelding from one of my neighbors – a half Appaloosa and half mustang. This gelding was five years old and very high strung. The woman I bought the horse from was afraid of him – he was too much of a horse for her to handle. When I would get on to ride him, he would immediately raise up in front and try to buck me off. I talked to a horse trainer about how to break him of this bad habit. He told me to get a stake or rubber hose, and when he raises up hold the reins very tight and hit him between the ears as hard as I could. Eventually, he got the message. Once he almost hurt my leg by rubbing me against a tree. After I rode him up the mountains a few times, he became a better and better horse. He was a little stouter than Chief, and very quick. I had to be constantly on my toes. After a few years, he became a good mountain horse, but nothing compared to Chief.

Chapter 11

PESKY, PESKY WOOD TICKS

In all my outdoor adventures, the worst thing I have confronted are those little, not very noticeable, wood ticks. I have picked up my share of them and have had quite a few embedded in me. When hiking off the trail through grass, they attach themselves onto the pants and then they crawl up your leg until they find a desirable spot to attach themselves under the skin.

The Lab here in Hamilton (U.S. Public Health Service Laboratory) was testing the bugs and encouraged people to bring them in after they had been embedded – not breaking the head off as you pried them loose. It had to be done very carefully. I brought quite a few to the Lab.

On one occasion, after I brought the wood tick in, I received a letter from the Lab a few days later that the wood tick was not infected. There are three diseases you can catch from a tick – Rocky Mountain Spotted Fever, which is the worst, Colorado Fever, and Tularemia, which is very rare.

After I received the letter, I started to feel very weak, my eyes hurt, and I had a high fever. I called the Lab and explained how I was feeling and they told me to stand by. They would check for Tularemia and get back to me. Contracting Tularemia from a tick is rare; you can also catch Tularemia from skinning a wild rabbit if you have a cut on your finger.

A little while later, the Lab called and told me to get to a doctor right away because I had contracted Tularemia. I went to the see the doctor in a hurry, and he gave me two choices: have a shot, or take a few pills. I went for the pills. I was laid up for about 10 days until I started feeling better. Another time, I caught Colorado Fever and had a fever overnight, but was over it by the next day. Luckily, I have never caught Rocky Mountain Fever; it can be fatal but if caught in time one can recuperate.

Wood tick season starts when the snow melts in spring, and usually lasts until the end of June. After the first of July you are seldom bothered by them. Nowadays, I stay on the trail where there is not as much grass. I always wear tight pants over my shoes, but still catch one occasionally crawling up my pants, which I will take off my pants and grind into the dirt with my boot. This is my experience with wood ticks. I do not like them, but they will not keep me from hiking.

Mario with a moose taken on an Alaskan hunt.

Chapter 12

ALASKA MOOSE HUNT

All of my live I have loved to hunt. I enjoy the pursuit of the prey, as well as I love to eat the meat of game. Most of the time I have hunted close to home and for many years I applied for a bighorn sheep permit with the Montana Fish and Game Department so I could hunt for a sheep with my long bow, but I never had any luck.

During my first race, I met Z (not his real name). Z eventually participated in several of my races and I learned that Z also loved to hunt. We planned to go bighorn sheep hunting together by Big Sky in the Spanish Peaks area. Anyone could buy a tag for this area, so we bought our tags. We learned that there would be many hunters at opening day, so we took our rifles instead and I left my bow home. Fish and Game allowed only six sheep to be taken in that hunting district and as soon as the quota was filled, they would shut down the season. It would have been extremely hard to get a sheep with a bow since the animals were so spooked by the time the hunters on opening day started shooting. We were both lucky and each of us bagged a nice ram.

During this hunting trip, I got to know Z a little. We did a lot of talking. He told me of his problem of being bi-polar, which was not easy for him to disclose. He had gone into the service and when they discovered he had this problem he was discharged and put on disability benefits. He was married and had two boys. He was somewhat high-strung. He needed to be on medication but did not take it because it had so many side effects. I overlooked his disability. He was very energetic and never seemed to run out of steam. We started talking about going to Alaska on a moose hunt.

I found out from a few bowhunters in the Hamilton area about bowhunting in a very remote area of Alaska and I got in touch with an outfitter by the name of Jay Massey. My buddy, Z, and I would be floating the river Cheeneetnuk, which is about 100 miles long, with rafts. The outfitter would supply us with food, stove, cooking utensils –

all the provisions, including the rafts. And someone would pick us up at the end of the trip and collect the outfitter's stuff. But this was strictly a hunting trip for bowhunters and since Z did not want to hunt with a bow, but rather with a rifle, Jay suggested for us to choose a different hunting area.

This second option was a 120-mile-long float trip. The river itself was three different rivers merging in an area was very remote. The outfitter had floated this river just a couple of years before to check how navigable it was. He said it could be done but warned us it would be difficult. When he first ventured into this area, he used a super-light homemade four-wheel dune buggy to transport the supplies on a trailer two and one-half miles from the lake over the tundra to get to the first part of the small river, which actually was more like a creek. After several trips over the tundra, the machine got stuck so deep that he could not get it out. He just had to leave the trailer there. So now we would have to haul all the supplies and rafts – in all 700 pounds – all by ourselves, which took three days.

Z had bought a brand new Dodge pickup and we agreed to take his truck to drive to Willow, Alaska; he offered to pay for the gas going up and I agreed to pay on the way back. It took us three days to get there. Once there, we got in contact with a flying outfit that would fly hunters and fishermen with small pontoon planes, called Beavers, to remote spots over the Alaskan range, which Jay Massey had pre-arranged.

We arrived there on the 4th of September. One of the pilots could fly us sometime the next day, which was the 5th of September. The office was right next to the lake from which we would take off. Our supplies and dismantled rafts were waiting there for us, so we got busy loading the things into the plane. We landed on a small lake. The pilot got us as close to the shore as he could, but since the lake was too shallow along the shore, we had to put on our hipboots and carry all of our supplies and gear about 100 feet to the shore.

We set up a tent there. The weather was really nice. The following day, which was the 6th of September, we started packing our gear over two and a half miles of tundra to the beginning point of our float trip.

It felt like going over a sponge to cross the tundra. When we were carrying the heavy loads over the tundra with hip boots, it was very tiring because every step we were sinking in a foot. We learned to stay on the grassy spots rather than the bare spots. The bare spots turned out to be like quicksand.

Our food had to be kept on an elevated platform, which our outfitter had built, so the animals, mostly bears, could not get to it. A piece of tin-like stove pipe around the tree kept the bears from climbing up. As we looked around, we saw a good size bull moose as well as some cows, grazing on the nearby hillside. We also could see several bears gorging themselves on huckleberries, which were twice as big as we have here in Montana.

In three days we finally had all our stuff by the creek and were ready to start on our first leg of the journey. It was now the 9th of September. The rafts were pumped up, the supplies were split in half, and we each had our own cooler. At first it was very difficult to float on the small creek. At times we had to take the rafts out and drag them along the creek bed to avoid fallen trees and rocks. It did not help that I had very little experience in floating. I had practiced only with a friend on the Bitterroot River for about an hour.

It took us most of the day to float about a mile and we decided to set up camp for the night. That evening it rained all through the night and we discovered our tent leaked and by morning our sleeping bags were soaking wet. We had a couple of tarps along and from then on we put them over the tent. We fixed clam chowder for breakfast. We tried to eat the heavy canned foods first. We also had along a cookstove, two gallons of gas for cooking, pots and a frying pan. We had a axe and a small handsaw so we could chop wood; and in case we should punch a hole in the raft, we carried a repair kit along.

On the 10th of September we set our rafts into the Gagaryah River, which is about 50 miles long, to continue on our adventure. Even though this river was a little bigger than the creek we'd begun on, we still had to fight a lot of fallen trees. When we would see a logjam ahead, we would jump out of the rafts and pull them onto shore to get around the trees, one raft at a time. As we floated along it was easier to navigate since the river had picked up more water from other creeks.

We floated for three hours. We could see several big bear tracks in the sand along the shore. We pulled onto a gravel sandbar and set up tent. While Z was starting the fire, I was preparing the food for our meal. I had brought some of my own groceries along from home. I was cooking potatoes with Walla Walla onions and ham. Z drank coffee; I had a couple cups of wine.

After the meal, Z went on a little hike along the river to look for moose. He took his .475 H&H rifle along just in case of a grizzly bear encounter. He also had a .300 Weatherby, but did not think it was big enough to take down a grizzly since he had read how ferocious they could be, so he had left it behind. I had my longbow along and also a 12 gauge Model 88 Maverick O.F. Mossberg shotgun for bear protection.

I only hunted in the mornings, never in the evening because should I happen to hit a moose and he would not go down right away, I might have to track him a ways. So I would do chores in the afternoon and gather wood, and in the evening I would take time to write the events of the day down.

Z and I had agreed that he would help me call in a moose since I was trying to get one with the bow. The weather was actually a little too warm, 35 degrees during the night and around 70 during the day. If the weather would be colder, the moose would come into rut and be easier to hunt. This country was very wild and remote; not another human around, just Z and I, but even here the silence was sometimes broken by low-flying jets breaking the sound barrier. Somewhere out there was a base from which they tested these planes. We cussed them out – they scared the tar out of us!

Z and I got along fairly well so far, but he had a bad habit of smoking a lot. He had started smoking at 11 years of age and was now 37. He had tried quitting several times, wore the patch, and even went to the hospital to get some help, but to no avail. So far we had a lot of rain just about every day. The river was rising. The night before it must have been 10 and 12 inches, bringing the water up just a few inches from the tent. We watched the river closely. Jay Massey had advised us that if the river should rise, we would be better off to stay put until it came down. So we were wondering if we should wait a couple of days on the gravel bar, waiting for the rain to stop, or if we should take a chance to move our tent on higher ground into the timber.

This part of the country was heavily timbered with tag alder trees 15 to 20 feet high, so we decided to take a chance, loaded up and headed down the river. We were looking for a higher gravel bar. It was around noon and had been raining on and off all morning. The river was now running a little faster. Some big boulders were sticking up out of the water, but we would not see how big they were under the water until we were right upon them. Z high-centered his raft on one of those rocks but managed to get it off without damage.

About an hour after we had taken off, we could see a gravel bar three to four feet higher than the water. We felt it was safe there to set up camp. The landscape was opening up, and we had a view of mountains around us about 3,000 feet high. We had a few more showers during the afternoon and we were really getting tired of all the rain.

The next day, which was September 12th, we had a little frost on the ground. It was cloudy but not raining. We went on a hike to look for some moose. We tried not to go more than a half mile from the river so we would not have to pack the meat so far if we should get a moose. We began making a few calls. Z was carrying his rifle and I had my bow along. We waited around to see if a moose would come in. Our visibility was not more than 50 yards because of the bushes and grass, as well as trees. All of a sudden, we heard a bull grunt. It sounded like he was a little ways off. We made a plan that Z should go 50 yards behind me and make a few more calls as well as breaking a few branches to entice the moose.

I was waiting motionless behind a few trees. A few minutes later we heard the moose coming toward us and I got a glimpse of the bull. He was 50 yards away from me. Slowly I brought up my binoculars to look him over. He was around a 60-inch class – a nice animal! It would have been easy to kill him with the rifle, but he needed to come 25 yards closer before I could take a chance to shoot it with my bow. My heart was pounding very fast. He stood there nearly a minute staring in our direction. Z called him in a few more times. He became suspicious and began circling us. He came up to 40 yards and then stopped. "Boy, what a handsome dude," I thought. But he must have gotten our scent and then walked back from where he came. I decided the next time I would go alone hunting because of Z's heavy smoking. I have to give Z credit; he was very fit and hard to keep up with. His passion was hunting. We followed the moose for a while but could not catch up with him. We went back to camp.

Z then went out to do more hunting. I tried to do a little fishing but had no luck. I saw some black bear. We never saw grizzlies at this particular area. No rain on this day. Z came back and told me he saw a bull moose, but since it was not a very big one he let it go and wanted to hold out for something better.

September the 13th the weather was good. We were going down the river again. I always say my prayers before we take off to ask the Lord for protection. I was finally getting the hang of rafting but when I heard the river rushing loudly, I always was getting tense. We had been floating for an hour and 15 minutes when Z pulled over with his raft onto shore to have a smoke.

We had quite a ride with all the big boulders in the river. It was very difficult to avoid them. Twice I high-centered on rocks. We always had our hipboots on so we could jump in the water to pull off the rafts which were high-centered on a rock. I then had to jump fast into the raft because the current was very swift and one mistake meant bye-bye raft. I held very tightly onto the rope just in case.

I pulled along Z's raft and he motioned to me that a caribou was crossing the river. Z said he would take the animal and waited until he reached the shore. Then he shot it. The caribou was about 150 yards behind us. It was a nice bull. We got it and quartered it and then put it in the raft. We had to drag the raft upstream to where the caribou was shot.

We were hoping to get two moose that close to the river, which would be great. I took some of Z's supplies in my raft while he took the caribou. Down the river we went again.

Half an hour later we pulled up onto shore and set up camp. We hung the meat between two trees and then cooked some caribou steaks for dinner which were very good but a little chewy. In a few days the meat would be much better. Z went for a hike with his gun. When he came back he hit me with the news that he was out of cigarettes and that he had actually planned it this way! I did not want to believe this and asked him, "You're kidding me, aren't you?" "No, I thought it would be a good time for me to do it now," was his answer.

Had I known this ahead of time, I would not have gone on this trip with him. I could see trouble ahead, and it was going to be hard on both of us. I was very disappointed in him for doing such a stupid thing and I told him so. He was upset with me. From this point on, my communications with him were strained.

September the 14th, after breakfast we went out hunting – splitting up. I made a big circle of about two miles making calls but did not get an answer, nor did I see anything. I came across someone's old deserted camp. I could see utensils, an old enamel bowl, a rusted out cooking pot, as well as various pieces of deteriorated clothing laying on the ground. I picked up the utensils and bowl and took them with me. I could not help wondering what might have happened; maybe someone died here a long time ago while hunting. At 12:30 I came back to the camp. Z was there and we ate lunch. Afterwards we crossed the river with my raft. We wandered around to find some moose but all we saw were some old tracks. We came to a small creek with salmon swimming in it so we went back to camp to get our fishing poles. We both caught a salmon about twenty-six and a half inches long. At camp we cooked one of the fish on the grill but it was very musky and it did not taste good.

We had been told that after September 15th they would be no good to eat. They were right. We burnt the fish in the fire but the smell of the burning fish drew hundreds of bull flies. We had to build a bigger fire just to get rid of these nasty flies. It was a relief when the flies finally left after the fish and smell were gone. Z was beginning to eat more food, especially sweet stuff. His frustration over not having a smoke was mounting.

On September 15th we crawled out of our sleeping bags at 6 a.m. It is raining again. We got the fire going and 20 minutes later it stopped raining. We packed up and headed down the river. The river was now flatter and higher and easier to navigate. We hoped it would stay like this for a while. But we had to be alert for tree "sweepers". When we saw a sweeper, we paddled backwards in order to slow down somewhat, but our efforts made us look like a duck coming in for a landing. Sometimes the swift current would pull us right into the tree. What a nice wild river this was. Very clean and pristine. It was a privilege to be on such a beautiful river.

It started raining again. As we floated along we stopped every so often to check for signs of moose. A young bull moose crossed the river in front of us. We pulled over and set up camp. It was three o'clock in the afternoon. This area looked like good moose country. We had seen some rubs and fresh tracks. Then we built a good hot fire to dry ourselves.

Our food supply was diminishing fast. We had some beans, rice and ham left, and I cooked it all up. We ate this "goulash" with crackers and, since we were very hungry, it was not bad tasting. Then the tent sprung another leak, so we had to cover it with tarp again. It drizzled all day long.

On September 16th it was raining again. We ate caribou meat since we were running out of regular food. While we were eating breakfast, a moose came within seventy-five feet of our camp. He did not look fifty-four inches wide so he was not legal to shoot. We needed colder weather and snow instead of rain, which would cause the moose to come into rut. The last few days it was 35 at night and between 70-80 during the day. We were waiting for a break in the weather.

Not being able to smoke, Z was eating like a horse. At this rate, we would be running out of food before the end of the trip. Z had brought some sugar from his home and Jay had also supplied us with a pound of sugar, which Z had in his tea. So now he was out of tea and he started to drink coffee instead.

The rain finally quit. Z went out hunting and I started to make some stew from the heart of the caribou. I put in a can of tomatoes and the last of the spaghetti. Raining again. I went out hunting for a while and made a few calls but nothing showed. I walked along the river and picked up some interesting pebbles

On September the 17th we woke up to a frosty morning – 30 degrees and cloudy. For breakfast we ate the last of the stew. After breakfast I hiked about two miles along the river, made few moose calls, but nothing showed and I returned to camp around noon. When out hunting for moose I use two different calls. One is a grunt call to attract the bull moose. If this does not work I make a cow call which sounds like a lost heifer.

I went to the river fishing and caught a salmon again but threw it back in. We had been told these rivers were full of graylings, but we did not see a sign of them. We were getting hungry for a change in our menu. Hopefully, we would catch some further down the river. We had very little food left. Z came back to camp. He had seen a big bull moose but he was a long ways off and did not come close.

September 18th. Caribou steaks for breakfast again. We finally had a nice, clear, frosty day – 25 degrees. We packed up again and rode down the river. We floated about half an hour, pulled to shore and set up camp. Z spotted moose near our camp. He grabbed his gun and headed toward the moose. I walked over to the spot just to see the moose walk into the woods. I needed a bath desperately, so into the river I went without soap to do a little scrubbing. At 7 p.m. it was about 70 degrees. The little bugs were really bad. I had to spray myself with bug spray from head to toe.

On September 19th Z went hunting again. Z absolutely could not relax. He also complained about a sore back. We had two hindquarters of the caribou meat left, which we always hung between two trees. That had to be done when we set up camp so we would have some meat left the next day. Evidently, Z hurt his back when he took down both quarters at once and carried them to the raft. We were sitting by the fire when he told me that. I told him he should have shouted to me and I would have come to help.

It was 9 p.m. and I was ready to turn in when I heard a moose raking his horns in some brush just a little ways from camp. Z also heard it. He grabbed his gun and walked toward him. I was right behind him. We were within forty yards of the moose and he looked right at us. Z was ready to take him down but I cautioned him not to shoot in the dark, which is against the law. The size of this moose looked legal. I did not want to argue with Z so I kept my mouth shut. He shot the moose in the chest. The moose just turned around and headed toward a wooded area by the river. We went toward the river hoping to see him cross. We waited five minutes but the moose did not show up. Z went to get his flashlight and go to the spot where the moose was shot to track him.

Meanwhile, I kept looking down the river with my binoculars. All of a sudden I could see horns floating down the river and I saw the moose was laying to one side. The current had taken him down the river. He disappeared around the bend. I called Z to come over to tell him what I had just seen. I told him to use my raft and he got into my raft to cross the river; his raft had all the caribou meat on it. We had not seen any trees that day to hang the meat up in. It was easier to walk along the one side of the river, so Z walked. Pretty soon he came back and announced that he had found the moose but needed some help. I took my knife along.

We went back across the river to where the moose was laying – but he was not there anymore. The current took him further down. By now, it was pitch dark. I suggested to forget finding him now and to wait until morning. Not Z. He was bound and determined to look for him further down the river. He had his gun with him. I had not brought mine, just the flashlight. I went back to my raft feeling a little uneasy, thinking about all the bear tracks we had seen earlier in the day. I went back to camp.

A little later Z came back on the other side of the river and I rafted over to pick him up. He did find the moose but it was in deep water. But the water was cold and the meat would keep. We tried getting some sleep but mostly just tossed and turned.

We got up early on September 20th and drank some caribou broth and coffee. Z was anxious to get the moose and took off with his raft. After I had broken camp I followed him. What a sight! The moose was laying in two feet of water with nearly a sixty-inch spread – quite a trophy. Z was already busy gutting him out. We had our work cut out for us.

There is a saying – don't shoot a moose in the river. Z did not shoot him in the river, but he ended up there. The Alaskan moose are huge and almost as big as two elk together. We had a hard time gutting him out because of the cold water. We cut the moose in half with the axe and we managed to drag the halves to the edge of the river so we could skin him. Z wanted to have the head mounted so we very carefully skinned the chest and the neck. We cut his head off at the neck, leaving to cape out the head for later. I was counting on boning out the meat to eliminate a lot of weight. It would be so much easier to handle it because we would be at least another four to five days on the river. I was willing to pack half of the deboned meat into my raft. It would be so much safer rafting without the extra weight.

Even the river played a big factor. Z, however, was not about to bone out the meat. I felt he was using poor judgment and I knew it was going to be a disaster down the river, but I helped him put all his meat in his raft. It was 5 p.m. when we started floating again. Z was ahead of me so I could watch him. The raft looked overloaded. Rafting behind him seemed the right thing to do in case he needed help.

The stretch we came to looked like ideal moose country, and I also wanted to get one. So I hollered at Z to pull over and set up camp. He tried to pull over but I could see he was having problems. I pulled up alongside him and noticed something was wrong with the raft. Worse than that, we were heading for some rapids. We had to pull over real quick!

I got ahead of Z with my raft and pulled mine onto shore. "I sprung a leak," Z shouted, "and the raft is sinking very fast." He jumped out of the raft and between the two of us, we barely managed to get the raft close to shore where it was shallow. All the meat was wet. We could not camp out on this spot but we could see a gravel bar about 100 yards down from us.

We had to unload everything – the meat and all – into my raft. We had to make a couple of trips until we had everything on the gravel bar, including his raft. We pulled my raft with a rope along the river. Then we set up camp on the gravel bar and looked at the damage to the raft.

We patched the hole but it had to dry eight hours before it could be pumped up with air. As it was getting dark by now, we were setting up a fire. All of a sudden, as we were breaking the sticks, a moose was coming in to check things out.

"Go ahead and take the moose!" Z shouted. "You can use my rifle," I said. I had come here to get a bull with my bow and besides it was getting too late to shoot. I told him to leave it alone and I would go after it in the morning and hopefully I would get him. But Z took off anyhow to look for him.

He came back a little later and said to me: "You should have seen him. I got very close to him. He was bigger than mine." Now, I lost it! I said to him, "You are an idiot!" and I was really mad because I had just a few more days left before the closing of the season and it was my turn to try and get one. He got so mad at me for calling him an idiot that he started to jump up and down. At this point I thought he could kill me, and I actually was afraid of him, so we called it a day.

The next morning, which was the 21st of September, I decided to go hunting in the morning until noon and after that I would be done hunting. I just could not go on like this. I informed Z about my decision and asked him again to bone out the meat by the time I was coming back. I told him I was willing to take half of his meat in my raft. Altogether he must have had between 800-900 pounds of moose and caribou meat in his raft. Even Jay Massey had suggested to bone out the meat and had given us some clean sacks to put the meat in.

I went out in the morning and made a few calls, but nothing showed up. The big moose had been spooked. Around noon I came back.

Meanwhile, Z had packed everything in his raft except for the two hindquarters of the moose. He wanted me to help him put the two quarters into his raft. I pleaded with him to please not do this – it was a matter of survival. But he ignored me and managed to get the meat into the raft by himself.

He was ready to go. We divided the rest of our food and he took one of the big canvases. After looking at the big map that Jay Massey had given us one more time, he said, "I'm leaving, see you down the river".

I was really worried about him. He did not know what he was

getting himself into. I spent the night at the camp alone. I figured he had his moose and caribou and was anxious to get home and was not really interested anymore in me getting my moose.

The morning of September 22nd I gathered my gear together and headed down the river. This stretch of the river was very nasty – logjams and sweepers blocking the channel in every direction. I had to get out of the raft quite a few times and pull around the debris. It was a struggle and my raft was not even that heavy. I was thinking of Z and the problems he must have had with his raft and all the extra weight. I was alerted to a big log jam ahead in the middle of the river. As I got closer, I could make out two channels: one to the left and one to the right.

It looked like I could squeeze by the logjam on the left side. The right side did not give me a clear vision into the channel. I pulled in my oars and let the current take me through the tight spot. As soon as I got by the logjam, I spotted Z's raft upside down in the river with all the meat and the moose head in the water. Z was standing along by the bank under the canvas trying to dry off; his clothes hanging on branches for drying. I pulled over. He was pretty shook up. Then he told me what had happened.

It had taken me about a couple of hours to get from the last camp to the log jam. It had taken Z a lot longer with his heavy raft. It was dark when he got to the logjam, and he could not see to go ahead any more. Unfortunately, he took the right channel. Suddenly he could see a log lying all the way across the channel about two feet above the water. He managed to duck under, but as soon as he lifted his head a huge snag loomed right in front of his raft. It punched a big hole in the raft, releasing all the air. The raft then turned upside down and all the contents ended up in the water. Z got tangled up in the ropes and almost drowned.

We had life jackets along; I always wore mine but he chose not to do that. I had warned him about the dangers of not having his lifejacket on. His valuables – gun, camera, etc. – everything was wet, and the caribou meat and horns were floating away. He was very hungry and wanted to know if I had any food left. All I had left was a can of tuna in water and half of the moose tongue. He knew I had a coppa left, which is similar to salami and ham mixed, and wanted some of it. "Let's save it for now. We are not out of the woods yet," I replied.

He ate the tuna and I had the moose tongue. We also cooked up a little moose meat. It was very sandy from laying in the water and we had to trim quite a bit off. While we were sitting there, he confided in me and said that if it was not for hunting, or, if his wife would leave him, he would commit suicide. He was also afraid to go down the river the next day. I put my hand on his shoulder and told him we would make it together and that this time I would take the lead.

Between the two of us, we had enough patching material to cover the big hole. We had to let it dry before we could put air into it again. I set up the tent for the night, we gathered some wood, and then just sat around. In the near distance we could hear three different wolf packs howling; it was an awesome experience to be out there in the wild enjoying nature and beast. It gave us a good feeling.

I tried to be calm so not to agitate Z. We also boned out the meat earlier in the afternoon and put it in the sacks so we would have it ready for tomorrow. I was hoping we would make it to Stoney River Lodge without any problems the next day.

At 7 p.m. it was still sunny. We had a little shower but it did not last very long. Standing around the fire and talking, Z broke down and cried. He told me more about his illness. He said, "People wonder why I don't have a job. They don't understand. I just can't. Once I had a job in the past and I got so tired of correcting everybody's mistakes. I always liked you because you accept me like I am, until this trip. You said I was not responsible. It really hurt me. Everything that I did on this trip was not to your satisfaction."

I replied, "I made an effort to compromise and I am not always 100 percent right either. Two heads are better than one, is my motto." By now, I was also very emotional and started crying. After he told me all this, I had a better understanding of him. We finally called it a day and crawled into our sleeping bags. We wondered when we would hit Swift River. I figured we were very close since we were coming out of the hills and the terrain was flatter.

On September 23rd, early in the morning, we looked at the map and could identify a round hill standing out in the flats all by itself. We could actually see this knob from our camp, about a half a mile away. It was about 1,000 feet high. According to this, we were only about two and a half miles from Swift River. We felt relieved.

We had a little breakfast consisting of six tablespoons of granola in hot water, and coffee. The wolves were howling again – the call of the wild. After we broke camp, we divided the meat and loaded it into our rafts. We started floating down the river. We hit a couple of rough spots but nothing as serious as what we had been through. Then we said goodbye to the Gagaryah River.

A few bald eagles were flying overhead as we entered Swift River. So much water! Some places the river was a half a mile across. The snags were fewer and we had more room to navigate round the bad stuff. Also the river was much smoother and no more problems, I thought.

That morning when we had pumped up Z's raft we noticed a small leak at the corner of the patch that we had glued on. We barely had enough to overlap the big hole. Every two hours we had to stop and put more air into the raft. At 10 a.m. we got hit with a very strong wind blowing against us. We had to row very hard and it was very tiresome.

For four hours we bucked this wind. My left hand was getting numb. We took turns leading when, at 2:00 p.m., Z was ahead of me when I saw a tent at the bank of the river. I shouted, "Hello!" and a man came out, the first human being we had encountered in eighteen days. "How far is it to Stoney River Lodge from here?" I asked. I thought he said twenty-five miles and thought that, maybe if we pushed hard, we could make it later tonight. A little later a boat came speeding by heading down the river. At 5 p.m. we saw a cabin alongside the shore. We pulled over. An Indian man with a boy came out and greeted us. He invited us into his little cabin. He and his family lived at Stoney River Lodge. This was his place for hunting and fishing. We could see a boat nearby. We also met his wife and young daughter. They had six children but the others were at their house. We found out that it was still forty miles to Stoney River Lodge and we realized we still had a long way to go.

Z gave them some moose meat. The meat had been in the water three times and was very sandy – not really too good for human consumption anymore. The Fish and Game Department required that you bring all the meat with you and should you give some away you had to give proof of it.

This was the third time the moose meat from Zee's moose ended up in the river. By this time, the meat had spoiled.

The last few nights we had a full moon. We were hoping for a full moon night again. This way we could travel during the night. The wind had finally calmed down – what a relief – so we took off again.

All of a sudden it dawned on me that we should have asked the Indian at the cabin to take us down the river the rest of the way. We would have paid him, of course, but it was too late now. I was in the lead and Z was about 200 years behind when, suddenly, the river split into two channels. I had to make a quick decision: right or left. I took the right fork and knew I had to pull over real fast so I could wave at Z to let him see on which side I was going.

I waited there about five minutes to see if he would come through. Then I thought that he must have taken the other channel. I went back into the raft and headed down the river to where the channels would be merging. I could not see him so I waited there for a little while, but he did not show. I was concerned. Maybe something had happened to his raft. I decided to spend the night right then and there.

I had no food left except the coppa and I snacked on it with a little coffee that I made. The next morning, September 25th, I packed up and paddled down the river. Shortly thereafter I reached the Kuskokwim River, which is the second largest river in Alaska. The river was very wide; lots of water heading down toward the ocean. I could see the current in the center of the river moving very swiftly. I could have traveled faster but was afraid to go toward the center. Instead, I chose to stay close to shore. I was worried about Z, wondering if he traveled through the night and maybe was ahead of me. About an hour later I could see a few cabins on the hillside ahead of me. I noticed two guys standing by the shore so I pulled over. I asked them if they had seen a guy come by with a raft. I told them how we got separated last night, but they had not seen anyone. They had a little boat with a motor so I asked him if he would take me to the channel. I wanted to go back and make sure Z was okay. I offered to pay him, and he agreed.

I left my raft there and jumped in his boat. We took off like crazy. He knew what he was doing. I lay flat in the boat because it was too cold to sit up. We went to the channel where Z should have come through. We also checked some other smaller channels. He was not there. I figured he rode through the night. We went back to my raft and I found out it was only ten miles to Stoney River Lodge. I offered to pay him if he could take me and my things to Stoney River Lodge and he went for it. We loaded everything into his boat, including the raft, after I had let the air out and worked it into a bundle.

In half an hour we were at the Stoney River Lodge. I spotted Z right away talking to an Indian. I went over to him and said I was glad that he was safe. I had been very concerned about him. He did not seem very impressed and then the Indian said, "Is he the guy that would not haul the meat for you?" I said; "Listen, Z did not tell you all what really happened back there."

Z then told me that he had floated through the night and had he not seen the little light at the lodge, he would have floated right by. I wanted to find out about a restaurant, but how disappointing as there was none. Only about 15-20 families lived there. One white man and his wife lived in Stoney River Lodge – he was a teacher for the children in the area and he was the only one with a little plane. The Indians themselves used the river as the road if they wanted to go somewhere. I paid the Indian $100 for his services, and it was well worth it.

Z mentioned to me that there was a woman in the neighborhood who would cook up some food for me. I was very surprised – she had a very nice and clean house. She motioned me to sit at the table and she would bring me some food. Guess what? Caribou meat again! It was a stew and it was very tasty, as well as bread and butter. I was very hungry so I spread butter on my bread, which I never do at home. I gave her $10 and she was happy with that.

The Indian took Z to the place where he could call the pilot. It was around 4 p.m. Z talked to the pilot and he was not sure if he would be coming that evening. He said if he was not there by 5 p.m. that he would come the next day. At around 5:00 he showed up. He wanted us to load our personal belongings into the plane right away, and then tomorrow he planned to return for the horns and bags. All of a sudden, we were surprised by a slushy hail shower, which lasted about five to ten minutes. We were ready for take-off. The pilot, for safety reasons, climbed onto the wings and with his bare hands he scooped off the slush which was about 2" deep. It was too dangerous to fly like this. It was not an easy job. An hour later, we landed after a bumpy flight at McGrath. The pilot had a little hanger and office and he allowed us to leave our stuff there for now.

I walked over to a restaurant – the only one in town – to get something to eat. Z walked to a place where he could make a reservation for Anchorage and from there to Willow, where his truck was parked. The owner of the restaurant and bar was a big, heavy lady. She also had some rooms for rent. She was doing the cooking and a fellow was behind the bar. I sat on the stool and asked the lady about something to eat. The lady said she was very busy right now, which I could see, and said to come back in an hour.

It was then that I made up my mind that I was not going home with Z. His behavior was unpredictable and he was accident prone. It was

Sunday evening and Marc Air and Alaska Air were the only airlines flying out of here, so I strolled over to Marc Air which still had the office open. The girl informed me she had one seat available on Tuesday night. She recommended that I check Alaska Air in the morning; they might have a seat open earlier. Close by was a bar so I had time to kill some time and I entered the bar and ordered a glass of beer. I was very hungry and thought they might have something to eat as well. The bartender said he had only a microwave hamburger, and since I was desperate, I went for it. What a mistake! It was plain awful. I then headed back to the restaurant, but still had to wait a little longer.

Meanwhile, I inquired about renting a room. Yes, she had rooms – $70 a night with two beds. The room was not the cleanest, and it was dingy. Z asked me if I would pay for it. I thought Z might be running out of cash so I said okay. Later I asked him if he was a little low on cash. He said no, which surprised me.

The owner was finally caught up and I wanted to see a menu. She said the only thing she had was rib steak and french fries – take it or leave it. It sounded wonderful, and I hollered "I'll take it! I'll take it!" While she was cooking, she told me her husband just had left her and I could see she had her hands full. One of her little girls was sitting in a high chair, eating spaghetti. The little toddler took the bowl of spaghetti and dumped it over her had. I said "Mama Mia! You like-a the spaghetti, huh?"

Off to the side was a small room with a couch and a TV inside. A little girl was laying there on the floor watching TV. Once in a while she would come out into the kitchen or bar to visit and to see what was going on. The owner had quite an overwhelming job which I could observe from the counter where I was eating. The meal turned out to be very good. I turned in at 10 p.m. Z was still hanging out in the bar.

The later the evening, the louder the music became. It was very noisy and difficult to sleep. After 2 a.m. it quieted down, some. Z finally came to bed at 4 a.m. I had been wondering if he had started smoking again.

On September 26th I got up at 7 a.m. and went down for breakfast. Since I was one of the first ones, I was served right away. I filled up on pancakes, bacon and eggs with coffee. It hit the spot. I owed the lady $7.00, but I give her $9.00. About that time, Z walked up to me and I informed him that if there was an opening on Alaska Air I would be flying out of here. I would not be going back with him. He got mad at me and said I could not do that. I answered him that I had enough and like it or not, I was going. I told him when he got back to Montana to give me a call so that I could pick up the things that I had left in his truck and that

I would settle up with him for what I owed. Then I went over to Alaska Air.

I had to stand in line for about an hour because other hunters were checking in and they had prearranged flights. When I finally reached the desk, the lady had one seat left and told me the plane was leaving in 15 minutes. It cost me $900 for the ticket. I ran across the runway – 200 feet wide – as fast as I could to gather my gear. The flight attendant saw me struggle and came halfway to help me. I brought my stuff to the office for weighing and wanted to box up my shotgun and bow, but there was not enough time. I ended up taping the gun and bow with heavy-duty tape onto my luggage. The girl at the desk did not reject it because the plane was ready to take off. She called someone to take my bags over to the plane. I was concerned the way my gun and bow was fastened to my bag, hoping all would arrive safely in Missoula.

After boarding the plane, I felt so relieved that I was finally on my way home. All of a sudden it hit me – I had left two shells in the magazine in the gun! I was so stressed out that it bothered me all the way home to Missoula. In Anchorage, I switched planes to Seattle, then to Whitefish and then on to Missoula. I arrived there September 27th at 1 a.m. My wife and daughter were waiting for me at the airport.

I went to pick up my baggage – the two bags were there but not the gun or bow. I hurried back to the desk and reported it. I found out that my gun was in Seattle and that they had discovered the two shells in the magazine. I had to fill in a form and the person behind the desk promised he would call Seattle and explain my circumstances – and why I made such a stupid mistake. A few days later I received a form from Seattle which I had to fill out and explain again what had happened. I also apologized for the mishap. Then I called Seattle; they wanted me to call Alaska and Spokane as well. Finally, my gun arrived back in Missoula, but there was no sign of my bow.

I called Z's wife and left a message for Z to call me after he got home so I could settle up with him and pick up the rest of my things from his pickup. Later, I met with him, paid what I owed and gathered my things. When we departed, Z said "I'll see you" and I said, "Goodbye." I never got my bow back. On top of that, I had to pay a hefty fine for my mistake. But, even though I had a lot of aggravation and big expenses ($3,500 just for the outfitter) and no moose, I was thankful I had come home alive. I found out later that Z and his family had moved to Alaska because he loved to hunt so much.

Mario on top of Uhuru Peak, Mount Kilmanjaro in Africa.

Chapter 13

KILIMANJARO

I met Skip Horner about twenty years ago when he was putting on a slide show about Kilimanjaro, Africa, for a benefit at the local high school. His profession was guiding people to the top of some of the tallest mountains all over the world. I could see how beautiful the mountain was from the slides. Some of the most beautiful flowers, and the vegetation on the lower part of the mountain was astonishing. He later signed up for one of my Endurance Hikes. During the hike, I asked him about climbing Mount McKinley or Kilimanjaro. I was already over sixty years old then. I wanted to know his opinion – could this old guy still tackle McKinley? His response was that I was very fit and should not have any problems at all.

During the winter, we occasionally went alpine skiing in the Bitterroot Mountains with my oldest daughter and some other friends. I knew he had been guiding groups up on Kilimanjaro for the last twenty years, so I inquired about going on a trip with him and that I was very interested in signing up. He was willing to give me a discount of $500 when I signed up. The government of Tanzania did not allow individual climbers to tackle the mountain. You had to have a guide as well as another guide from Tanzania, who would hire some young kids (from fifteen to twenty years old) to carry all our supplies up the mountain. They also took a cook tent along, including table and chairs. They prepared all of the food for us. The reason why we had to hire all the "locals" was to provide some income for them since they are very poor there. This was all prearranged by Skip.

At the end of December, we flew to Nairobi and spent the night there. Our group consisted of seven climbers – four of which were doctors. The next morning we were picked up by a fellow with a van that Skip knew. He took us to a small village at the base of the mountain. We spent a night there as well.

The next morning, we all drove to the trailhead of Kilmanjaro. The kids grabbed all the supplies – including our personal gear, tents, chairs and table – and started to head up. We slept two in one tent. All the kids, about fifteen of them, slept in one tent. They had no sleeping bags and lay on the ground close to each other to keep warm. I was amazed to watch the kids carry all the stuff – either on their heads or their shoulders since they had no backpacks. It seemed very awkward, but they were used to it. They were actually hard to keep up with and always ahead of us. The scenery was beautiful. We even saw monkeys in the trees.

The weather on the lower part was nice and warm. Once in a while we had a shower, but it did not last long. It took us five days to get to the top.

We usually hiked about four or five hours a day. The highest camp was at around 15,000 feet. From there on, we had another 4,000 feet to reach the top. We took off at 1:00 a.m. the next morning from our last camp. One of the climbers dropped out at this point – he had a bad cough. The kids did not go along, but waited there for us to return. Only the leader came with us. One of the doctors was getting altitude sickness.

Near the top of Kilimanjaro, we could see several glaciers about fifty feet high. There were rumors that they all would be gone in fifteen years and the locals below were concerned about the water supplies diminishing.

Four of us made it to the summit at 5,895 meters. Two of the other doctors made it to Gilman's Point at 5,685 meters. The view from the top was spectacular. While I was on the top of the mountain, I asked one of the three guys that made it with me up there, to take some pictures of me spreading Jack's ashes, as well as me doing my headstand with the American and Italian flag, one sticking out of each of my boots.

A group from Greece was on top of Kilimanjaro also and they were watching us. One of the men came over and asked me how old I was and I gave him my age. He then pulled out a bottle of booze from under his coat and offered it to me and said, "Take a sip, you deserve it!" Many people from all over the world climb this mountain. I was amazed to see all the trash from the upper half to the top of the mountain.

We started heading down to Gilman's Point to meet up with the rest, and then head further down. We reached the camp around noon and we fed lunch. I gave my rain poncho to the young kid that hauled my personal bag up the mountain. I also handed my left-over chocolate to the kids. As I was hiking down, I heard three guys who were heading up talking in Italian. I had to say hello in my native tongue. They were surprised to meet up with another Italian. We visited for a few minutes, took some pictures, and went our separate ways. As it turned out, they were from Bergamo, twenty miles from where I was born.

We hiked about ten miles down that day, which was the hardest part of the whole climb. We finally made camp and stayed overnight there. The following day we hiked all the way down to the Park Service station. We had to take a different trail going up and coming down, and we had to check in with the Park Service people at the end of our climb. I received a certificate that I had made a successful climb to the top of Kilimanjaro and one of the head bosses of the Park Service signed it.

While I was waiting for the rest of the gang to come down, I was bombarded by vendors wanting to sell souvenirs, etc. I did buy a book about Africa. I then spotted a stand selling beverages. I went to buy a bottle of beer and watched the woman take the cap off the bottle with her dirty hands. The beer also was very warm. They, evidently, didn't have any ice there. About an hour later, after I had drank the beer, I got the runs and I ran as fast as I could to behind some trees to take care of the situation. Skip, along with the rest of the crew, showed up. He settled up with the other guide and kids.

Our adventure package included a stay at two different lodges. After the climb, we were picked up by a van and driven to Serena Lodge, which is close to Lake Manyara, for a two-night stay of relaxation. The Lodge and the layout surrounding the Lodge, was fantastic. It was owned by a white man and his staff were all colored servants dressed in uniforms. The food was delicious and served smorgasbord style with lots of variety, anything you could want. We only had to pay for the liquor. The Lodge surroundings were just gorgeous with beautiful trees and flowers. Many, many birds were singing in the trees. We could even see little monkeys running through the grounds but we were not to feed them.

I inquired from one of the waiters how much they get paid a day for working at the Lodge. She told me only $1.00 a day and room and board. I was surprised to hear how little they got paid. She said it was so much better than being in the village and getting nothing. The facility for the night was a room for me and the other climber, with a shower, toilet and a mosquito-net covered bed.

The next morning we went into the dining room for breakfast. It was still pretty early. Skip informed us we would be going on a safari to view the wildlife in an open Land Rover. I told Skip I was not feeling well and not going along because I still had diarrhea. Skip did not listen to me and told me that I was going with them, even if he had to drag me! I was glad I did. I started to feel better and I enjoyed the drive to see all kinds of animals in the wild, up close. I took many pictures.

Around noon we came back to the Lodge and had a fabulous lunch.

It was suggested that we go see a native village about ten miles from the Lodge, so we could see how they lived. We took them up on the offer and someone drove us there. Each of us had to pay $15 to the natives in the village; however, we gave them $20 – it was worth it.

We were amazed at how the natives lived. They all lived in round huts which were about twenty feet in diameter. They had one bedroom with animal hides on the floor for sleeping for the man and wife, and a smaller room for the children. For cooking they had a ring of stones in the center, and used branches and wood. In the ceiling was a small hole for the smoke to escape. No windows -- just a small entry opening. The roof was plastered with cow pies and every ten years the roof had to be replaced. Some of the men had more than one wife. As was the custom, the men had their middle upper tooth pulled out and they also had a scar on one side of their cheek.

There were about twenty to thirty people living in the village. There was only one young man there who spoke English. He was the chief of the tribe. He had gone to Nairobi to get some schooling a few years prior, and they were now in the process of putting up a nice little building for a schoolhouse so the kids could go to school.

The village was surrounded by a three-foot-high hedge made out of thorn bushes to prevent the lions from coming in during the night. They owned a few cows, but they had to be constantly watched day and night so the wild animals would not get to them. They have had several confrontations with lions, and they fight them off with spears.

The women were sitting in an open space on the ground trying to sell trinkets made out of wood, some bead necklaces, and other things that they had made. They were very persistent and practically begged us all to buy something. We all bought a little souvenir from them. The men did a tribal dance for us holding their spears. The people are extremely poor; no electricity or running water. The water had to be carried from a spring. An old blind man was just sitting there on the ground – a very sad sight.

I had brought 300-400 writing pens with me and told the chief that I had forgotten to bring them along and had left them at the Lodge. He said he would send a couple of boys to the Lodge to pick them up. We went back to the Lodge later in the afternoon. Shortly thereafter, a couple of boys showed up to pick up the pens. They were very grateful.

The next day, we were driven to Tarangire Lodge. On the way to the Lodge I saw a woman washing some clothes in murky water in a small ditch alongside the road. It had rained the day before and she took advantage of the water. We also saw a woman carrying a bundle of sticks on her head. She must have come from a long way since there were no trees to be seen for several miles. We made it to the Lodge sometime during the day. They had little cabins where we would spend our night. The food that they had prepared for us was very good. A climbing buddy and I saw a river close by the Lodge and we wanted to go down and check it out. We sort of made a little loop back to the Lodge. There were big, huge trees, called Baobab trees, in this area with spreads of around thirty feet. The elephants love to eat the lower bark of the tree, which does not hurt it.

A couple of the women servants, who were about twenty-five years old, spoke a little bit of English. They asked me questions about America. They asked me if I was married and I said no. One of them was really interested in coming to America and offered to get married to me! I discouraged her and said that I was too old for her. I found out the word for "grandfather" in their language is baboo, and I told her I was a baboo. She would not give up and insisted I was still strong. I told her that when I got back to America I would try and get a young buck for her. She gave me her address but I threw it away since I did not want to get involved.

The next day we were scheduled to fly home from Kilimanjaro Airport, which was closer than Nairobi Airport. On the way to the airport we stopped off at a huge building. They sold a lot of beautiful artifacts and antiques, most of the made by the people from all over Africa. The natives brought all their stuff there to be sold. I was astonished when looking at the different things they had made. It took a lot of labor and time for the engravings on the beautiful wood. I bought a Kilimanjaro shirt there. In the entry of this beautiful building there was a handsome colored dude standing dressed in his best native outfit. He looked like a big chief of a tribe and he could speak English. He told me that Bill and Hillary Clinton where there and the Clinton's had someone take a picture of them with him. Later in the afternoon we arrived at the airport and took off to Amsterdam, Holland. Skip stayed behind. He had some business to take care of and would come home a few days later from there back to the U.S. on a different plane.

This was a successful, fun trip. It was a piece of cake climbing Kilimanjaro compared to McKinley. Here are the names of the other climbers that went with me: Steve Hoverman, Al Saletta, Steve Barr, Joe Sena and Don Potter, all from California, and John Cirtley from New York.

This photograph of a Rocky Mountain Goat taken by Mario from close-up range, actually within a few feet, gives one an idea of the extraordinary skills Mario exhibits in terms of both mountain climbing and wildlife observation.

Chapter 14

THE OLD GOAT CLIMBS DENALI
(Completes his 50 High Points and Becomes the Oldest Man on Record to Reach the Summit)
(As told by Cathy Locatelli)

The evening of July 5, 2004, I was awakened by a call from the Alaska Mountaineering School with the news that my father had reached the summit of Mount McKinley (Denali) that evening, and that he was doing very well. After the call, I phoned everyone that I knew would want to know. My eyes teared up as I went to sleep, thinking of the talks we had shared during our own hikes, his wishes if he didn't make it, and the training schedule he had formatted for himself.

Faithfully, he packed 50+ pounds of water at least three times a week, climbing local mountain-tops, and thinking of all he could to without to travel light on his journey to Alaska's highest peak, and the last mountain to achieve his goal. I fell into a relieved, joyful, sleep. I truly "know" my father. I have watched him accomplish feats that cannot be explained by a 140 pound man. Determination, will and desire is all I can come up with. He has taught me and proven to me that you can't let your mind talk you out of something. If your heart says you can, by the grace of God and your desire, you can.

He made the 20,320 feet peak in sixteen days, starting from 7,200 feet. Though the statistics say that the round trip is thirty-two miles, it is actually a distance farther since the climbers pack gear to various elevations and go back down to the lower camps – acclimating themselves for the elevation changes. The weather was good during his expedition; though extreme differences, the temperature did not go below zero at night or above 90 during the day.

How fortunate he was to have found a climbing partner, Pierre Terrault – a fifty-two-year-old French Canadian from Quebec. He had committed to a private expedition versus the trip Dad cancelled with a younger group of eight that began almost three weeks prior. One climber died, and two were badly hurt in a rock slide on "Windy Corner" on the way down from the summit. They came into Dad's camp in the morning he was to move up to the 14,000' camp from the 11,000' camp. They were, understandably, downhearted as they regrouped and continued for home.

Dad, Pierre, and guides Zach and Tim, continued to the 14,000' camp that day and acclimatized there for three days, then moved up to the high camp at 17,200'. After a night's sleep, they went for the summit and made it in sixteen hours. The wind picked up, so after Dad's headstand with the United States and Italian flags and photos, the team started their descent back to the high camp. The wind blew hard all night until about noon the following day. I asked him what his worst event was and he said, "That wind whipping against my tent all night, pushing snow against me and making the space even smaller. I could not sleep. I asked myself what I was doing here. I could be having a nice meal. Though, I was so happy to be done, I felt homesick."

They packed up camp and continued their descent to 14,000' where they spent the night and most of the next day until it was cooler and the traction on the snow would be better. Three groups worked their way down together. High temperatures and lower elevations made the trip slow and hazardous. Several climbers fell into crevasses – but no one was hurt. Dad felt that the trip down was more tiring and hectic. His chosen time was the last trip of the year for the climbing company. The last teams on the mountain pack out the remaining supplies that are cached.

Most Unusual Event – One group that was digging in the high camp found a human foot. It was that of a climber forty years prior that had told his expedition that if anything happened to him and he couldn't make it, to bury him on the mountain. He had gotten sick and died. His companions put him in his sleeping bag and buried him as he had told them to. He had been there, frozen, for all those years. His family told authorities to leave him on McKinley, where he wanted to be.

Biggest Disappointment – Dad says that he did not like being roped up the entire way. He is used to being on his own. The safety is more important, of course, but he says that it is very stressful when you are told to slow down and when you feel you might be too slow. Though hiring a guide greatly reduces your risk, he wasn't used to the rules and company policy that goes with it. He had purchased the lightest pair of climbing skis available for the trip and he knew that he could make better time both up and down using them. The guide company would not let him use them. He tried to convince them to cut him loose, to no avail. He had to leave the skis and rent snowshoes. He said that Kilimanjaro was a piece of cake, and all the mountains that he had climbed throughout the United States in one-day summits were a lot of fun, but Denali was different. More of an opponent, not as fun, but gracious during his time.

Best Event – Dad's final piece of the puzzle is in place, as he puts it. The oldest man prior to him on record was seventy-one years old also, but two months younger, and had climbed to the summit in 1982. Mario Locatelli is the oldest man on record to summit Mount McKinley – a bonus.

Congratulations, you old goat. So proud of you!

Climbing Mount Hood in Oregon.

Chapter 15

CLIMBING MCKINLEY

In the summer of 2002, Dusty Wood, Steve Biere and I decided to go to Wyoming and climb Devil's Tower. It turned out to be a successful climb for the three of us and it took six hours. I was really glad that I had been doing fifty pull-ups every day for many years because it gave me the strength in my upper body to hoist myself up on the rock wall of the Tower.

I joined the High Pointers Club in 2003 when I was seventy years old. The club's members try to climb all of the fifty highest mountains in the United States; the club is now twenty years old and has over 3,000 members. The name of the man that started the Club is Jack Longacre. He died in 2002 of cancer and was only sixty-four years old at the time. Before he died, his wish was that his ashes be scattered on the fifty highest points in the U.S., and also on some of the tallest mountains of the world. The lady in charge of the disposal of the ashes, also a High Pointer, is Jean Trousdale.

I had scattered some of Jack's ashes on Kilimanjaro in Africa in 2003. I also had planned on bringing some of his ashes on to Mount Everest, but I did not find anyone to sponsor and finance me. The trip would have cost $80,000. Had I been younger I could have teamed up with younger climbers and could have gotten away with $30,000. At my age, I was better off to go with a reliable outfitter, so I called Jean to find out if she wanted me to send the ashes back to her. I then suggested that I could scatter the ashes on Trapper Peak, which is the tallest peak in the Bitterroot Valley in to the Selway-Bitterroot Wilderness, and she gave me permission to go ahead. The wilderness, which is almost in my own backyard, is the biggest in the lower forty-eight states.

I had one mountain left to climb – McKinley in Alaska, the toughest one of all. It would be the last piece in the puzzle. After inquiring about which outfitter to chose, I decided to go with Colby Coombs, who operates a guiding and mountaineering school in Talkeetna, Alaska. I decided to take him up on the challenge.

He lined me up with a younger group of guys and then called me back a few days later. He had gotten a call from a fifty-year-old French-Canadian man and he told Colby that he was a slow climber. Colby suggested that if we were willing to pay a little more money he could give us two guides – Zach Shleser, and Tim Hewette. Zach had been up on McKinley only once the year before, and Tim was a newcomer and had never been up there. Both of them were about twenty-five years old and weighed about 190 pounds each. They also were very fit. There was also another fellow that worked for Colby and he wanted to climb with us, a man from New Zealand.

The climbing season on McKinley is from May to July. We flew from Talkeetna to Camp Kahiltna Glacier, which is 7,200 feet high. There were six camps along the way up and we spent one night at each camp, except at 14,200 feet where we spent three nights to get acclimatized. Colby had sent me a book on McKinley which he had written and I was asked to read it before I went on this trip. I paid special attention to his suggestion that one could use snowshoes or a light set of skis. He also required a physical exam by a doctor from me so he could be sure I was in good physical health for this trip. I also needed to bring twelve pounds of snack food along and he would supply the rest of the food. Jim from the Pipestone Sports Store in Missoula lent me his sleeping bag, a special suit and glasses, as well as some other items suited for very cold weather. He himself had been on McKinley and had first-hand experience with the conditions. That helped me out a lot and I did not have to buy all the gear.

He recommended that I could take some light skis along and this way I could ski up to 14,200 feet since I had done a lot of alpine skiing. I went ahead and bought a light pair with skins from him.

When I made it into Talkeetna on June 19, 2004, I met the group. Colby checked all my gear and supplies. My two quart-size water bottles did not have insulators so I had to rent two from him. Then he saw my skis and told me I could not take them. I referred to his book and told him I was a very good skier and before Zach and Tim were born I had already done alpine skiing for many years. I became very upset – just because the Frenchman could not ski I was not allowed to take mine. I argued with Colby, especially after I found out the guides were using skis. I told them, "Just turn me loose and I will stay behind and follow." Nothing could make Colby change his mind; they did not want the responsibility in case something happened to me. I had to rent some snowshoes and a pack from Colby as well since he did not like my backpack.

The day before we had to fly to base camp we had to show up at the office of the National Parks Service in Talkeetna to pay a fee of $150 each and then were briefed on the dangers of the mountain.

We started going up June 22. This was to be the last group of climbers going up the mountain for the season. The previous groups that had gone up before us left their unused supplies along the way. They would dig holes two to three feet in the snow, put the supplies in, and cover the holes with snow. Light bamboo sticks with markings of the outfitter's name would then be stuck in the snow by the hole so that other groups from the outfitters could find the leftover supplies. The extra food was stored there in case of a storm and they had to stay put until the weather improved. Other outfitters did the same with their own markings. The reason why the stuff had to be dug in at least two feet was because of all the ravens trying to find the caches and dig them up. We did not have to carry quite as many supplies with us since we would use some of the ones left behind from previous groups by our outfitter. Our pack that we carried was forty pounds and we all pulled a sled with provisions behind us.

We spent one night at our starting camp 7,200 feet on Kahiltna Glacier. That evening we practiced what to do in case one of us should fall into a crevasse. From 7,200 feet to 7,800 feet is a five-mile walk with many crevasses. The next morning, the 23rd, we woke up and in the afternoon we reached the 7,800 camp. We had to probe the area before we set up camp to make sure we were free of crevasses.

The weather was good but very smokey. Apparently there was a fire somewhere below in the valley. It was smokey until we reached the 14,200 camp. The next morning, the 24th, we headed to a camp at 9,700 feet. From then on, the climbing was getting steeper. We made it to 9,700 feet and set up camp there. There were five or six other groups of climbers present; a couple of them from Colby's outfit. The guides prepared the food but we also helped. The Frenchman and I slept in a very small tent together. We had to put our clothes and shoes on sitting down when we were getting dressed in the morning. In this camp, we spent an extra night.

On the 26th we got up very early to get ready to go further up the mountain. Just as we were getting ready to take off, a group of Colby's arrived, coming down. It turned out this was the original group that I was supposed to have gone with. While traversing Windy Corner, which is around 13,000 feet, they had a major rockfall. Very unusual. Three clients were injured and one was killed. A helicopter had to come to pick up the injured. It made me realize I could have been one of them. The two guides and remaining client were very shook up from the experience. It also affected us. We proceeded toward Windy Corner. Before we actually arrived there we set up camp nearby at close to 13,000 feet.

On the 27th we moved higher to reach the 14,200 camp. We spent three days at this camp to become acclimatized. Quite a few other groups from different outfitters camped there as well. It was sort of a rest area for acclimatization or spending the night before climbing down. The National Park Service stations would have a dozen individuals who volunteered. Several tents were set up; one was set up as an emergency tent for first aid in case someone was hurt.

While we were hanging out at this camp we learned from the National Park Service that one group of climbers at 17,200 feet were digging a hole in the snow to stash some supplies away before they went on. They hit on a body, which turned out to be that of Gary Cole, who had died there in 1969 from HEPE. The body was brought down to 14,200 feet but the family asked to leave him up there because he wanted to be buried on the mountain in the event something happened to him. The exact burial site was not disclosed.

We left our sleds at the camp and starting climbing to 17,200 feet. It mostly was very steep and several sections had ropes set up for us to clip with a mechanical ascender. A mechanical ascender is a tool you clip on the rope and it is attached to your climbing harness with a sling. It helps you to pull yourself up the rope. It took us most of the day to reach 17,200 feet. We set up our tents there and the environment was very harsh there. Previous groups had cut out snow blocks between three to four feet high and stacked them around their tents as protection from the harsh winds. We were fortunate that there were a few available so we put our tents right inside. We spent two nights there to acclimatize before going higher. Luckily we did not have a storm sweep in while we were there. It was a cold place to be.

Early in the morning we started our climb toward Denali Pass – 18,200 feet. We had to side hill over to the pass. This section had ropes mounted for us to clip in. Quite a few people have gotten badly hurt or killed on this particular spot. One could easily lose footing or balance and there was nothing to hold onto. It went straight down the side of the mountain. This stretch was about one mile across. From then on it was more of a gradual climb.

We came to a section that is called Football Field, a wide snowed-open area. The weather was not bad, a little windy, but very cold. Just half an hour before we reached the top was another small section of side hill and we had to clip in again. We had all our extra clothes on. The guide carried a shovel. We had to be prepared in case of a white-out. The two guides also each had a sleeping bag along so we could get two-by-two in a bag to keep warm. Even though we had our water bottles in insulators, by now the water that was left was frozen.

When we finally made it to the top, which was the 5th of July, the wind was beginning to pick up. We congratulated each other – it was a happy moment for all of us. As soon as we reached the top, Zach called Colby to tell him we had made it. I told Zach to tell Colby to call my oldest daughter, Cathy, to tell her we made it.

I handed my camera to one of the guides and asked him to take a picture of me doing my traditional headstand. It was not that easy considering all the clothes I was wearing, the blowing wind, and I was getting a little fatigued. We had disconnected our ropes since it was fairly safe and no crevasses were around. The actual top was semi-flat – about twenty by twenty feet. Zach wanted me to rope up again before I could do my headstand since the mountain on either side was very steep. I refused and told him I'd be okay. I had brought two small flags along: one USA flag and the other was Italian. I pushed them into my boots and then did my headstand. Zach was standing right close by in case I should fall. Everyone took pictures of each other.

The wind was getting stronger now and Zach said not to waste any more time but to head down. By the time we arrived back at camp 17,200, the wind was blowing very hard. It took us sixteen hours to the top and back. We just snacked on some food and then crawled into our sleeping bags, trying to get some sleep.

The wind was howling so loud we did not get much rest. We were glad to have those snow blocks around us. By the time morning came, the wind had blown a lot of snow on the side of our tent and it squeezed us and made our space in the tent even smaller.

The wind blew hard until noon. We all had a snack. One of the guides had brought a small stove along, on which we would heat some snow so we would have some water to drink. Zach gave the green light for us to pick up and head down to the 14,200 camp. We arrived at camp by nightfall. We rested up through the night and most of the next day.

When we were hiking up high, it had started to warm on the lower part of the mountain, which had softened the snow and made it hard to walk on. We waited until evening for the down climb, after the snow had hardened up. We picked up some caches along the way since this was the end of the season and the last trip of a group of hikers. We tried to pick up all the supplies left behind – as many as we could carry – and actually had more weight coming down than going up.

A group of Colby's with two guide and four climbers left from 14,200 camp before us, climbing down. We passed them when they had stopped to rest at 11,000 feet. We kept going to camp 7,800. Everybody in our bunch was bushed, so we rested a couple of hours. The guides set up one of the bigger tents so we could all be out of the wind. We laid down and waited for evening when the snow would firm up. The other group caught up with us and they went on down. We had a couple of words with them. After a while we followed on down also.

Since the weather had gotten pretty warm at the lower altitude, we noticed many exposed crevasses. We had to be very careful and went back and forth, as well as around, to avoid them. In spite of it, you could not always detect them because some of them were covered with snow. At one spot I actually slipped into a hole about two feet deep or so. I hollered to the guys in front of me to pull on the ropes and I made it right out.

We caught up with the other bunch again just in time to see the guide that was leading the group fall into a crevasse about two or three feet deep. We all went alongside the guide and Zach grabbed him by his backpack. We all had to back up to keep the tension on the rope, which made it easier to lift him out. Our group was getting very, very tired, but we kept going most of the night.

Around noon the next day, we made it back to the starting point. A lot of commotion awaited us when we arrived into camp. While we were up at 14,200, we watched the Park Service people closing down for the season: helicopters flew in and out picking up tents and other supplies to bring down to Camp 7,200. Now we could see them flying in and out with all the supplies that were not needed anymore. Three big black Army helicopters landed then to pick up all the supplies, which were brought down from the 14,200 camp. We had to wait a couple of hours before it was finally our turn to be flown back to Talkeetna.

Chapter 16

MOUNT EVEREST

Right after I climbed Mount McKinley in 2004, I felt good enough to tackle Mount Everest. However, it took $80,000 to climb Everest and I needed to find someone to sponsor me. I was looking for a person or company who had the means to do this, so I called the editor of *Outside Magazine* to see if they would publish my intentions – but they turned me down. My daughter, Cathy, e-mailed Oprah hoping that she would have me on her show with my skis on and I would do a headstand and also an eagle spread. I was hoping to catch someone's eye who might think that this old guy might pull it off and thus support me. They replied that once a year they have a show about the "American Dream" and they were going to let us know, but nothing ever came of it. The story of my attempt to find a sponsor was also published at the time in the *Missoulian* and *Ravalli Republic* newspapers in Montana.

Larry Peterson, the head nurse of Life Flight at Saint Patrick's Hospital in Missoula, read about my plan. Since I had contributed some money for Life Flight and Saint Patrick's House in the past, they got together and sent me a check for $500 for my climb of Everest. However, by the time I realized that my plans would not come true, I called Larry Peterson and explained the situation to him. I could either send the money back to him, or I could add the $500 toward the proceeds of a race that I was in the process of lining up. I wanted to raise some money for the firefighters who had lost their lives fighting fires in Montana so they could put up a memorial in the Stevensville City Park. He agreed that it would be fine with him, so that is what I did, so their donation ended up going for a worthy cause.

Mario with Dusty Wood of Woodside, Montana, on top of Mount Elbert in Colorado.

Chapter Seventeen

FAMILY AND FRIENDS

Cathy Locatelli
Hamilton, Montana

I was born one year and two days after my parents' wedding, which was on Valentine's Day. We always had enough land with our home to have lots of animals. When I was very little, we had rabbits which I couldn't keep my hands off of. The big fig trees in the yard gave my Mom fits because I would eat so many. Dad drove a garbage truck then, he took me at least once that I can remember. He not only drove the truck, but the guys lifted the cans onto their backs and into the truck. Dad started to cut wood and sell it on the side.

Our next place was large enough for chickens, pigeons, sheep and for me to have my pony named AOK. I loved lying down in the long, moist rows of stacked wood that smelled of redwood, oak, and eucalyptus. They seemed to go forever and were great for playing hide and seek, and catching salamanders. It was easy to be alone within all the stacks of wood and the woods that we lived in.

Dad was always working and taught me to always be doing something productive when he was around. When he gave himself down time, it was almost always going to an 'all you can eat' smorgasbord on a Sunday, or camping out on a weekend in the mountains. We swam and fished. I loved jumping off the rocks into the river; Dad taught me how to swim like a frog and that almost any road was passable. I thought for sure we were going to roll down the mountain several times.

Dad and Mom would be fixing up one place to buy a better one. He became the largest wrecking contractor in Salem, Oregon, before we moved to Montana. We always had good food, nice clothes, and a neat place to live. I learned that hard work and determination were the key to success, more so than a college education. I still am in awe that a young girl from New Hampshire moves to Santa Cruz, California, and meets a young Italian from Berbeno, Italy, who could barely speak English, marry, I'm born, and now I live and thrive in such a beautiful place because of their tenacity and foresight.

Carlene Locatelli (1958-1989)
Written by her sister, Peggy

Having grown up with my sisters, they all hold many memories with me. My sister, Carlene, passed away in 1989. Since she is not with us to write anything in our father's book, I would like to share some memories I have of her and also mention what a truly special soul she was.

She was a wonderful big sister to me and I knew I could always rely on her if I ever needed anything. I remember when she took up square dancing and I can picture her now in the square dancing outfit my mom made her. She asked me a couple times to go with her, but I have to admit at the age I was then, which was about twelve or thirteen, I thought square dancing was for older people. However, she encouraged me to go so I went a couple times and stood in the corner watching people and snacking on the food. She kept trying to get me out on the dance floor and it took several weeks of going before I got up my nerve to give it a try. Once I did, it was a lot of fun. We went every week after that for a while.

She learned to be a pretty good cook, and I remember her coming home on the weekends from college and making bread along with a few Italian recipes. She moved to California and finished up her college classes and put her degree to use as a Psychiatric Technician. I enjoyed our long phone conversations while we were apart, and I flew to California one summer and had a great visit. We went to the Santa Cruz Boardwalk where we rode some rides, sat on the beach, and played in the ocean. I miss my sister very much, but I have comfort knowing I will see her again one day.

By her sister, Cathy:

Carlene died at thirty-one years of age. Carlene and I were almost three years apart. I was the oldest of four girls, Carlene was next in line. We had power struggles as most siblings do. She took piano lessons and had a knack for keeping things organized and clean. I seemed to take on the role of helping Dad outside and Carlene helped Mom with the house and kids. Carlene had some physical challenges that never seemed to keep her from achieving anything she wanted to do; she was the only one of us who went to college. Carlene had the biggest heart of anyone I have ever known. Before her passing, she devoted her career life to helping mentally retarded children, and her personal life to her husband Michael. Carlene was a courageous person who always wanted to help anyone she came in contact with. I look up to her; she makes me want to be a better person.

Angela Brown (born 11/23/61)
Great Falls, Montana
By Mario:

When I was in the wrecking business she used to run up to me when I parked my truck after my days' work and we used to skip back to the house together. She was an adorable girl. I remember one summer that I was particularly proud of her. She had raised a steer for 4-H and right before the big show day at the fair, the steer stepped on her foot when she was practicing her showmanship. It was badly swollen and she could hardly walk. She showed the steer anyway and received a Blue Ribbon.

Peggy Bowles
South Jordan, Utah

I am number four of my parents' daughters, born in Santa Cruz, California, in 1962. I was named after my mom, Peggy, and my middle name is Jeanine after my godmother, Aunt Giovonna. We moved from Santa Cruz to Salem, Oregon, when I was about five. We then moved to Hamilton, Montana, to a ranch where my most fondest memories of childhood took place. There was so much to do on the 160-acre ranch which included riding horses, playing in the creek, sledding in the winter, and of course, my Dad also put us to work helping pick up all the rocks in the field so he could grow and harvest hay.

I remember complaining about having to walk down our long driveway to catch the school bus, and Dad would quickly remind me of how many miles he would walk to school each day and how we have life easy compared to him until I became an adult and had my own kids. The one-liner I remember most is when I didn't think something was fair, he'd say, "Wait until you have your own kids.". I swore I would never use that line on my own kids but I found myself saying the exact same thing to my son, Branden, and daughter, Lindsay.

My greatest adventure would have to be when Dad took us girls to Italy. We visited my grandparents and met a few of my aunts, uncles and cousins. While there, we drove to France to see Dad's Uncle Giaccomo and his seven children, who were Dad's cousins.

Dad bought me a Brown Swiss heifer that I learned to train while in 4-H. I showed it at the county fair and won several ribbons. I graduated from high school and began my own life in Montana, then moved to Utah where I now reside with my husband, Todd, who was my best male friend for twenty years before becoming my husband. Montana will always be my home and I look forward to someday moving back and retiring there, which is years away but a dream I hold on to.

Carmela Uhlenkott
Lewiston, Idaho

As the youngest of Mario's daughters, I wasn't born until June 24, 1981, at Marcus Daly Memorial Hospital in Hamilton, Montana. On September 16, 2006, I married the love of my life, Toby Uhlenkott, and we are now expecting our first child. We live near Lewiston, Idaho, where we run Toby's family's Charolais cattle ranch. We enjoy spending as much of our summer as possible at cow camp near Weippe, Idaho. It reminds me of the Bitterroot Valley where I grew up – green meadows, trees, clear mountain streams.

These are the things Dad, and my Mom as well, taught me to appreciate. Absorbing the wild through spending tine in the outdoors fishing, hunting, hiking, camping and packing into remote areas on horseback. The skills and ethics that I have learned from Dad continually come in handy, and I look forward to passing them onto my children.

Some of my most treasured memories of time spent with Dad are from our hunting excursions, including deer, elk, mountain lion and pronghorn antelope. I continue to hunt here in Idaho, but it's not quite the same as being with Dad and hearing him say, "Ya got em!".

Bill Goslin
Stevensville, Montana

Mario Locatelli is one of the more remarkable outdoorsman that I have known. Imagine a native of Italy who knows the Bitterroot Mountains far better than most native Montanans. Imagine an avid skier, climber and hiker who is often old enough to be the father of his outdoor companions. Mario is the kind of guy who if he says he is going to do something, then he will do it – "no matter if it kills him". Few mountaineers can match Mario's cat-like agility across scree and talus slopes. If you think he is hard to keep up with going uphill, you would probably find him harder to stay with going downhill.

Since I spent some time in the Bitterroot Mountains, it was no accident that I met Mario. Once when riding a chair lift at Lost Trail Ski area, I mentioned finding a jacket dropped by a back country skier on Gash Point. The skier next to me said, "I bet the jacket belong to that Mario guy". A few more chair lift rides later and somebody said, "That has to be that Locatelli guy." It turned out he was not looking for a jacket but he was looking for someone else to ski with. Little St. Joe, St.

Mary's, Ward Mountain, Downing Mountain, Lolo Peak – all of these were not problem for this old goat in his late fifties. Apparently he would rotate through his ski buddies so he would not wear them all out.

Mario once asked me if I would walk through the mountains with him from Twin Lakes around the Twelve Mile drainage, across the head of the Camas drainage, over Ward Mountain, and down to Roaring Lion Creek. It sounded like a once-in-a-lifetime hike, so we went. The route was not always perfectly obvious. There were lots of uneven rock and no trail. Water was nowhere along the route. There was a short distance of narrow ledge with a 100' drop-off. The sun was hot and rain made for slippery footing. The scenery was great. Mario wanted my opinion. Would this twenty-five-mile plus route make a good marathon route? A competitive event? I told him he was crazy. Within a few months he held the first of many Mountain Goat Marathons along this very route.

Mario would look at maps and develop a desire to hike to and climb many of the higher peaks. When he was getting to the point, he did not like to sleep on the ground or pack a heavy pack but he felt an urgency about making it to the top. So he would find willing friends, twenty to thirty years younger and talk them into going along on one of his 'day trips'. To climb in one day MacDonald Peak – highest in the Mission Range, Mount Rainier – highest in the Cascade Range, or Granite Peak – highest in the Beartooths, requires extraordinary determination and stamina. No problem for Mario. Impenetrable brushfields, grizzly sign, unfamiliarity with the area, long approaches, exposure to steep dropcliffs, glacial crevasses, lack of sleep – the kinds of things that did not matter once you experienced the summit. Mario would be the one who would experience the summit standing on his head!

Here is how you might experience doing a day hike on Mount Rainier with Mario. Leave western Montana at 5:00 am. Drive to the National Park. Send Mario to get the climbing permit, which is never given to novices. "Are you experienced?" the Park Ranger asks, but then feel foolish after sizing up the callused hands, the full gray beard jutting from the firm jaw, the confident gaze, the Italian accent. Of course! Within a few minutes he is back with the coveted permit. Now it is time to grab something to eat and get some sleep in the back of the truck. Soon you are listening to Mario snoring like a baby, wondering if you too will sleep, but knowing you will be hiking by midnight. By 11:00 p.m. you are packing and snacking with or without sleep. First on trail tread, then on rock, then on snow you will climb without stopping from the base of the mountain to Camp Muir, the standard camp for overnight trips. At Muir, it is okay to lay down for a few minutes. It is quiet. All of the rest of the climbers for the summit have left. As you rope up, you see a snaking line of headlamp beams lighting up the snow above you in the otherwise near total darkness, with an impressive number of stars above. A stairway to heaven. This sight alone is worth the climb. With Mario, you are soon caught up with the last party. They slept at Camp Muir over 4,000 feet in elevation above the bed of your truck. As darkness gives way to the sunrise that is below you, groups of climbers politely give way to you and Mario. When climbers get backed up at a difficult spot and it is time to wait, you break out a bagel layered with prosciutto and fontina cheese. You have brought a little bit of Italy with you. There is a friendly camaraderie on the mountain. Perhaps a hundred people all with the same goal. Many of the other climbers quietly check out the guy with the gray beard. Before you know it, you are at the top, having passed most every group. The scale of the landscape is somewhat incomprehensible to someone who judges mountains by Bitterroot standards. You take a few pictures, knowing you cannot take it all in. You are visiting a place that surely would take your life should you stay. It is time to go.

A 9,000 foot elevation loss awaits you. This is where Mario is at his best, going downhill. You have a blinding, high-altitude headache. Never mind. Down through the glaciers, down through the snow, down through the rock, down through the glorious wild flowers. Keep going or he will be out of sight. Ibuprofen awaits in your truck. Your 'day trip' ends at 4:00 pm. You survived, but it is not over until you drive to the nearest town, more than an hour away, to find a motel and food. Here is the real test. Both of you are too tired to drive, but the body odor in the cab is so strong you cannot sleep. Somehow you stay between the lines and make it. A shower helps you feel ready to re-enter civilization. You walk in a daze to the restaurant. It is an ordinary town with ordinary architecture, but now everyday things appear very unreal. People seem like strangers. The blank smile of the waitress says she can't fully comprehend your experience, the effort, the scenery, the danger, the exhaustion. Truth is – neither can you.

Dusty Wood
Hamilton, Montana

Mario first knew me as that darn kid next door ripping around on my obnoxious motorcycle. He wondered how we could make so much noise 24/7. He called frequently to try to get me to go back country skiing or hiking with him. Finally, my buddy Colby and I – we were fourteen then – decided to snowshoe up Ward Mountain with him. We had to park way down low due to huge snow drifts blocking the road. I thought to myself, "this old guy must be nuts." He seemed confident we could make it, so away we went. He stopped to rest and let us catch up quite often, never resting long enough before we would hear the now so familiar "let's mosey" prodding us along. We finally made it to the top and I was hooked. What an awesome feeling of accomplishment. Thanks, Mario!

Naturally, we were ready to go again, this time with our downhill skis and boots on our backs to the top of Gash Peak. Over the next few years we skied all the best peaks in the Bitterroots. Just after my freshman year in high school, I made a mistake that changed my life. Drinking and driving – nobody was hurt, but to this day I don't touch the stuff. Needing something to occupy my time and energy, I got involved in the Ravalli County Search and Rescue. Mario was the rock climbing leader and a major part of the search efforts. Everyone in the unit gave their time and knowledge unselfishly, and I looked up to and respected each and every one of them. As rock climbing leader, Mario was responsible to train all of the new guys. My first training mission I will never forget. We went up above Mill Creek Canyon to do a Tyrolean Traverse. Mario asked if I would like to set up the anchors on a pinnacle across this seemingly huge, cliffy cut in the side of the mountain. Once again I thought to myself, "This old guy must be nuts". He seemed confident we could make it, so away we went. We repelled down to the bottom and snaked our way up the other side and watched Mario set up the anchors on top of the pinnacle, still thinking this is crazy. We proceeded back to the other side with the rope attached to the top. He set up the anchors on the cliff adjacent to the pinnacle, pulled the rope through, and tightened it with some knots that I've forgotten the name of. It worked! We all tied into the safety line and clipped onto the rope that was now stretched across the canyon and traversed across to the pinnacle. What a rush. I was hooked. Thanks, Mario!

We continued to ski, hike, climb and go on rescue missions together throughout the remainder of my high school years. I joined the Marine Corps for five years, which put a damper on my outdoor activities with Mario. But the weekend I returned home, he was running the last of the Mountain Goat Benefit Races and needed help at the 12 Mile Creek checkpoint. My dad usually helped out, so we went to man the checkpoint. Mario wanted me to race, but I felt a bit out of shape to do the 'Race', a treacherous twenty-five-mile race across the mountain from Twin Lakes to Ward Mountain trail head with several checkpoints along the way to keep track of everybody and make sure no one is injured or lost.

The race was a benefit to raise money "for those in need". Each year, Mario spent countless hours organizing the race and always seemed to find the perfect cause for the money to go to. That was the last race due to pressure from the Forest Service demanding permits and insurance; by the time these were paid there wouldn't be much money left over for the cause. But Mario, being as stubborn as he is, found that he could do a hike and collect donations instead of entrance fees, so the Mountain Goat Benefit Hike-A-Thon was created. These hikes were great. They all were still over twenty-five miles over the rugged Bitterroots with at least one peak climbed – four one time! Everybody traveled together at a moderate pace, which allowed more people to participate. There were twenty-five contestants along on the El Capitan/Three Como Peaks hike. What an accomplishment for one man to organize and pull off this type of event for so many years and miles covered, no less than 20,000, with no serious incidents.

Over the last twenty-five years, Mario has traveled all around the country, climbing mountains most people could care less about. They don't know what they are missing! Every trip was an awesome adventure that was far superior to the pain and misery. We always had a ball together and I loved every minute of it. Thanks, Mario!

John Klingbeil
Stevensville, Montana

    I first met Mario shortly after moving to Montana eleven years ago. I serviced his truck; it had plates that said "MTN GOAT" and I figured maybe he liked to hunt them. He invited my wife and I to go along on a mountain lion hunt with him and his dog. That's when I learned he *was* the Mountain Goat. He mentioned that he did a Hike-A-Thon each year as a local benefit and I said count me in, and promptly forgot all about it. A few months later I got a call from the Mountain Goat himself asking if I was ready to go. There would be a few hikes to see what kind of shape everyone was in. Then we were going to climb El Capitan and the three Como Peaks all in one day. At the time, I couldn't help but think that the old goad was maybe just a little bit crazy. After the first training hike, up and back down a rock fall up Roaring Lion, I was hooked – sore, but hooked. I struggled to keep up with Mario as he ran down the rock fall. He would look back and tell me to slow down, and then take off running again. Afterward, I knew why he was called the Mountain Goat. I also knew he was crazy and wished I had met him at least ten years earlier. The next day I could barely get up the stairs at work.

    I hiked the last two Mountain Goat Hike-A-Thon's before the Forest Service red tape and pressure finally go to be too much for Mario, and he set his sights on climbing all fifty high points in the U.S. By now, I knew him well enough to have no doubt he would succeed. One of many lessons I've learned from Mario is if you put your mind to something and don't quit trying, you will eventually succeed. That lesson was driven home to me when Mario, Dusty Wood and I tried to make Gannet Peak (Wyoming's high point) a day hike. When we mentioned our intention to the forest ranger in Wyoming, we got the usual "you people are crazy" look and were told it couldn't be done. We had every intention of proving him wrong. We came to the end of the twelve-mile trail before daybreak and had to wait awhile before we starting climbing so we could see the rocks. We were making great time as we climbed the creek bed we'd chosen as our route up the mountain. There was some water in the creek as it had stormed the night before. Several hours into the climb we needed to get across the creek, but fast-moving water, uncertain footing, no rope and the possibility of a long tumble over the rocks make it too unsafe to continue; Mario pointed back down. We spent an hour or so looking for another way around this area, but finally decided it'd be too late even if we did find a way. As we climbed back down to the trail and began the twelve-mile trudge back to the trail head, we were already discussing when we'd be able to try again. I was disappointed, but had learned another lesson, one Mario had obviously learned long ago – making it to the top isn't nearly as important as making it back down. A few weeks later, we went back and made it to the top by a different route, though we didn't do it in a day I'll still call it a success.

    Shortly after climbing Gannet, I went through a divorce and while I was able to mountain bike and hike my way through the summer months, as winter came I could feel some depression coming with it. I wasn't sure what I'd do to keep my mind in check. Mario had been through the same scene; he kept in regular touch with me and had asked me numerous times to go skiing. I though he was crazy, hiking up a mountain to ski back down; isn't that what ski lifts were for? What about avalanches, crashing into trees and rocks, and there was no grooming.... He kept trying and finally I went. I hauled my snowboard up Gash Bowl on snowshoes and had one of the biggest grins frozen on my face all the way down – hooked again. Each year since then I've purchased fewer and fewer lift tickets. What better way to spend a day than skiing with a mountain goat and a few other close friends knowing you earned your downhill turns?

    Over the past ten years, Mario and I have done quite a bit of hiking and skiing together, and while some trips have been a little more challenging than others, I have always had a great time and come back feeling just a little bit better and a little bit smarter. Mario has always been a great inspiration to me and has become a good friend also. I know he'll continue to inspire countless people to get off their butts and "mosey" as he continues to climb and hike and ski.

Skip Horner
Victor, Montana

I probably can't add much to the 'Mario the Mountaineer' mystique. That's the legend, and rightfully so. On Kilimanjaro, I was impressed with his attitude, which was that of a climber relatively uncertain about his ability. He'd never been to higher altitudes before and he wasn't sure how to do it, so he approached it as an eager beginner. He got very, very fit, and he took nothing for granted. He paid scrupulous attention to details like diet, sleep and footwear. He asked questions every day, just to be sure he had all the information he needed about the length and condition of the route. He was the perfect expert beginner. He knew the right questions to ask and he responded appropriately to all the new information. He was genuinely thrilled to reach the top, as if he wasn't sure he'd make it until he actually got there. No one else in our party was surprised, however, as he was certainly the most motivated and prepared of all. His handstand on the summit certainly shocked and delighted our African guides.

It was his charm that impressed me most, however. He acted so innocent and unabashed about everything. He loved Africa and found Africans to be as open and unaffected as he was. He engaged everyone he met in conversation, and their instant recognition as one of their own was evident in their reactions to him. He especially liked the African ladies, not surprisingly, and they liked him. On two occasions, while chatting with the lovely receptionist behind the desk at the hotel, I overheard them propose marriage to him! They actually asked if he would marry them! Each time he reacted the same, laughing, stepping back, and saying no – they really wanted his son, not him; he was too old for them. But no, they wanted him. I've never witnessed this before, but that was the affect he had on people. He was genuine, entertaining and self-deprecating; he was just the sort they wanted to spend their lives with. Never mind he was an older American who probably had money, there were plenty of those around. It was the charming African-ness of his nature they liked. Mario's legend is that of a mountaineer, but it's his charm that makes him so loved.

George Corn
Hamilton, Montana

My first back country ski in Montana was with Mario. To say that it was not quite what I expected is just a bit understated. It was the winter of '82. As a skier who had knocked around the back country in Colorado for a couple of years, I had a very high and totally undeserved opinion of myself as being up on the latest in back country ski gear, style, knowledge and coolnesss. The trouble was, I didn't know anyone that skied the "woods" when we moved to Montana. In fact, there weren't all that many folks skiing the local peaks and woods back then and local knowledge about access and routes was not easy to come by.

With a full-time job and family, I didn't have much time to explore on my own, so when a friend invited me to ski Little St. Joe one weekend, I jumped on it. Located mid-Bitterroot Valley, its broad, deep meadows and bowls dropping from a wide summit ridge clearly seen along the Bitterroot Range from Highway 93 had made it one of my main objectives. I set out on a January weekend, equipped with my best back country gear. I showed up at the trailhead, expecting to see a group of young hardcore types, as I thought of myself in those days. Instead, I saw a small guy of close to fifty, which was ancient to me at that time, along with a father about my age and his eleven-year-old son, who turned out to be Jim and Jason Kazebier. All three were friendly as all get out, and the oldster had a real twinkle in his eye and a ready smile, but I was put out. Oh great, I thought to myself in disgust, family day with gramps and the grandkids; this is going to be a trudge. We'll be lucky if we cover a mile today. No way are we going to get to the meadow with them. I mean, they're obviously nice folks, but no way are we going to get to the goods. And look at their gear, I thought, hiking boots and old cable bindings on beat-up downhill boards. Sure, I was on identical rig, but that was six years ago. That's so old school now. Cool folks in the know, meaning me, ski tele in the back country and carry cut-down grain scoops for avy work, not plastic shovels.

Covering my disappointment at what was clearly going to be a waste of one of my precious weekend days, I patronizingly resolved to take what comfort I could from the great snow, spectacular views and the good workout I would certainly get since it was obvious I was the only one fit enough to break trail.

But a funny thing happened. Heading up the ridge, the little old guy, as I thought of him that morning, somehow managed to stay out in front while breaking trail. Funnier still, I was having to work hard just to stay up. Surely this was a mistake. No question but this was just a spurt of short-lived energy to show off to the new guy. Doubtlessly he was going to fold within a few minutes. How could he be talking his head off and telling jokes that were actually funny when I was breathing hard just to stay up? Undoubtedly, dad and son would be begging him to slow down before that. There was no question I'd be up in front shortly, showing all of them how it is done and lamenting, in a tactful but condescending tone, that it was just too bad we couldn't get to the top of the ridge and those sweet meadows; but wow, what an effort they had given it.

Well, of course, that never happened. In point of fact, I think I even made some excuse like fiddling with a ski binding so that young Jason had his crack at breaking trail before I took my turn in the rotation. What did happen, though, was a glorious ski trip as we chugged up to the top. Mario continued telling his marvelous stories all the way up the peak about hunts and hikes in the Bitterroots and Sapphires. At the last pitch, which is awfully steep but thankfully short, Mario pulled out some of the best homemade sausage I have ever tasted and offered me some just out of pity as I munched the current energy bar of the era.

When we paused on the comb of Little St. Joe, Mario pointed out the various ways he had hiked, climbed, scrambled and skied just about everything we could see from there. North, south, east and west, our views were fields of mountains and I was thanking my lucky stars I had moved to Montana and found a friend who could show them to me. Also, by that time, tired as I was, I realized that I was in the company of an original, one-of-a-kind outdoorsman. This man not only loved the Bitterroot Mountains, he lived them. In all too short a time, the cold got to us and it was time to do what we had come for. After stripping off climbing skins and lacing up our boots, we pointed 'em down, turn after turn making the price of our effort up, cheap at twice the price. It was just us, turning our way down through those meadows and glades I had looked at for the last year. Mario always kept us on the best line and even had paths through the brushy pinch spots. It was a glorious day.

I would go on to enjoy many ski trips with Mario, and we were lucky to have Jim and Jason on many, too. Some were colder, some had better snow, and some had worse. Once we even did a pavement-to-pavement day ski of Trapper in midwinter, but none were more memorable than the day Mario introduced me to the Bitterroot's back country.

Joel and Nancy Bender
Hamilton, Montana

It was some god awful time of the morning – 3:00 or so – and Mario was calling, again.

"Hey Nancy, is Joel there?" Like, where else would he be. "Joel, are you going out? You should go out, there is fresh snow and for sure you will get a cat track." "...call me later." Click! Mario loves to run those cats and Joel was his "not so always eager to be out at oh dark thirty" accomplice. I would groan every time the phone rang at that time of the morning because it could only be Mario.

Hiking with Mario up past Mill Creek on one of the Mountain Goat Endurance Hikes, we realized one of our hikers was missing. After many more miles criss-crossing the mountains we headed back down toward the valley. We put in a lot of extra time and miles looking for him (he quit us but didn't tell anyone) and Mario was feeling personally responsible and quite upset at the thought of someone in our group missing. No matter the hikes or the races, Mario subscribed to the philosophy that the "devil's in the details". He wanted to assure himself that anyone coming on his strenuous hikes was up to the task. He knew his routes (although some were admittedly hiked some years prior) and tried to leave little to chance. Mario knows the mountains can be fickle, the weather can change suddenly and dramatically, and he was often willing to lead hikers he didn't know into areas that were very remote and potentially deadly. I admire him for that.

His enthusiasm for big and wild places enables him to convince others that they should be out doing that too! "Hey, you're young, let's mosey!" Then, of course, we do and we love it, and at the top of wherever we've taken ourselves, Mario does a headstand and we revel in the mountains and what we have accomplished in one day. Always in one day. There is, though, a conflict of feeling I think. As much as Mario loves to share those big and wild places, it comes at a personal sacrifice to some of his own enjoyment as he worried and watched everyone, always being sure we would all make it down safely. We are all indebted to him for giving us the opportunity to explore that view instead of admiring it from the valley floor – for many would not take the big step out the door to explore some of those high places on their own. Thanks, Mario.

Mario Locatelli is the original tough guy – old school to the core and when it comes to endurance races or hikes, he's always considered the harder the terrain the better. My relationship with Mario started in the early 90's with the Mountain Goat Marathon; watching him cross the rock slate and talus slopes effortlessly like a goat, I was amazed. He definitely set the course to his strengths – low center of gravity, lung capacity like a fifty-five-gallon barrel, and quick, small feet to dance across the rocks – the wilder and steeper the better. I raced Mario three times – hardest, toughest, and longest of my life and I never beat Mario! The best time he set when he won he was quite a bit older than me. He's definitely an anomaly.

With Mario, it's his way or the highway, but he has a huge heart and has given generously of his time and fund raising efforts back to the community. Somewhere there is a measure of energy expended per dollar raised and Mario's events would surely rank among the highest.

EPILOGUE

As of September 2008, Mario has bagged the toughest peaks in the Lower 48 for the second time, with the exception of Gannet Peak in Wyoming because of a snowstorm that blew in before he reached the summit. But he plans to make another attempt.

He's not sure he will go back to McKinley to reclaim his title as the oldest man to have reached the summit of McKinley (Denali, Alaska) in June 2004 at the age of 71½. His record was broken by a Japanese man in 2005 who was 72½. As of this date, Mario Locatelli is the oldest **American** to have reached the summit of McKinley, and because of the head-stand he does on every summit, his feet have been the highest of anyone's on McKinley.

"Take it easy, but go ahead. You too will touch what you reach for...." – **Mario Locatelli**

Additional copies of *"THE MOUNTAIN GOAT CHRONICLES"* may be purchased at $12.95 each, plus $3.75 for postage and handling, by writing the author at:

MARIO LOCATELLI
144 Mountain Goat Road
Hamilton, Montana 59840
Email: cathy@mtidlandco.com